"David Swanson takes a deep dive into the very formation process for white Christians—discipleship. This new and altered rediscipleship, designed under the influence of mentors of color, addresses structures of white supremacy, privilege, and segregation. Simultaneously, it reforms white Christians using the central structures of church life—worship, preaching, fellowship, and the like. I know Daniel Swanson. He has been thoroughly rediscipled himself before inviting others to embrace the journey he proposes."

Curtiss Paul DeYoung, CEO of the Minnesota Council of Churches

"There are few pastors I trust more to take on a major task like this. David is an astute theologian and is well trained and positioned to lead this conversation. Just as importantly, David is a respected and credible practitioner. He is highly regarded in the city of Chicago for his humility, his tenacity, and his commitment to first experiencing the necessary rediscipling in his own life. If you are a white Christian longing for a resource that will help you name where things went wrong and create a roadmap for how to get realigned with King Jesus, this is your book."

Daniel Hill, pastor, author of *White Awake*

"*Rediscipling the White Church* illuminates the worldviews and customs hindering white Christianity's witness. Swanson prophetically models how confession, repentance, and renewed minds liberate captive congregations and embolden them to holistically redefine discipleship. Through reimagined liturgical, spiritual, and ecclesial practices, this book offers a tangible framework for producing Christlike disciples who will in turn make Christlike disciples."

Dominique DuBois Gilliard, author of *Rethinking Incarceration*

"David brings a fresh lens not just in how to view the state of race in the church but how to address it. He integrates the practices of any congregation, including children, with God's call toward unity across race and toward addressing the systems of racial oppression in both the church and in the world. His emphasis on our communal discipleship is a great addition to the resources available to the white church to understand their history and role in reconciliation and justice."

Sandra Maria Van Opstal, founding executive director of Chasing Justice

"Having journeyed with David Swanson over the last decade, he has shown up and locked arms with people of color. David has learned that any approach to diversity that ignores discipleship simply rearranges the church furniture. In *Rediscipling the White Church* he offers a down-to-the-marrow look at how whiteness can be named and supplanted as a framing identity. Through reclaiming its rhythms, namely in its collective discernment and practices, he invites the church to reimagine itself through life in the embodied Christ. This book is incisive, winsome, and hopeful, and will be a gift to future generations of churches."

José Humphreys, author of *Seeing Jesus in East Harlem: What Happens When Churches Show Up and Stay Put*

"This book does not ask you to diversify your congregation. Instead it invites you to join the reconciled body of Christ. To that end, David Swanson has reimagined how to leverage the features of worship and service you already use—preaching, communion, children's ministry, evangelism, and more—to disciple the congregation you already have, regardless of its racial makeup. This is clear-headed, concrete guidance from a humble and experienced leader."

Brandon J. O'Brien, director of content for Redeemer City to City, coauthor of *Misreading Scripture with Western Eyes*

"If there is one book every Christian leader in America should read, it's this one. The wisdom Swanson communicates is hard won and applicable to ministries in any setting, not merely those in urban or racially diverse communities. Swanson deserves credit for approaching the entire subject though the timeless framework of making disciples, who obey all that Jesus commanded, rather than using divisive and fleeting cultural hashtags. Of course, not everyone is ready to receive this important word for our times, but whoever has ears, let them hear."

Skye Jethani, author of WithGodDaily.com and cohost of the *Holy Post* podcast

"David Swanson offers all Christians a gift in *Rediscipling the White Church*. He not only presents redemptive practices that white Christians might engage as discipleship pathways, he challenges white Christians by offering us his intellect and his story as sacred entry points into the work of confronting racism. The end is good news—Christ's reconciliation is an invitation wide enough and deep enough to save our lives and our communion."

Michelle Clifton-Soderstrom, professor of theology and ethics, director of the School of Restorative Arts, North Park Theological Seminary

"Let us *not* come up with more white solutions to the problems of white Christianity in the United States. Instead let us all follow a discipleship that shapes us beyond segregation, racial habits, and other cultural captivities to a new way of being . . . a way of being we call church. Allow David Swanson to lead us to the 'uncomfortable truth' that can free us to a whole new world of embodied solidarity as Christians of all colors. Read *Rediscipling the White Church* and awaken to discover Jesus at the center of a flourishing that includes all people in the Kingdom of God."

David Fitch, author of *Faithful Presence*, Lindner Chair of Evangelical Theology at Northern Seminary, Chicago

"I guarantee you will disagree with something David Swanson has to say in *Rediscipling the White Church*. That is exactly why leaders like me (and you) need to read this book! It is in listening that we learn and in exposing ourselves to dissenting opinions that we discover our own blind spots. For anyone who wants to learn and grow in their understanding of discipleship, race, and justice, read this book!"

Dave Ferguson, lead pastor of Community Christian Church, Naperville, Illinois

REDISCIPLING

**FROM CHEAP DIVERSITY
TO TRUE SOLIDARITY**

THE

WHITE

DAVID W. SWANSON

FOREWORD BY BRENDA SALTER McNEIL

CHURCH

An imprint of InterVarsity Press
Downers Grove, Illinois

InterVarsity Press
P.O. Box 1400, Downers Grove, IL 60515-1426
ivpress.com
email@ivpress.com

InterVarsity Press® is the book-publishing division of InterVarsity Christian Fellowship/USA®, a movement of students and faculty active on campus at hundreds of universities, colleges, and schools of nursing in the United States of America, and a member movement of the International Fellowship of Evangelical Students. For information about local and regional activities, visit intervarsity.org.

All Scripture quotations, unless otherwise indicated, are taken from The Holy Bible, New International Version®, NIV®. Copyright © 1973, 1978, 1984, 2011 by Biblica, Inc.™ Used by permission of Zondervan. All rights reserved worldwide. www.zondervan.com. The "NIV" and "New International Version" are trademarks registered in the United States Patent and Trademark Office by Biblica, Inc.™

While any stories in this book are true, some names and identifying information may have been changed to protect the privacy of individuals.

Cover design and image composite: David Fassett
Interior design: Daniel van Loon
Image: couple and children in church: © Lambert/Fotogrove/Getty Images
Author photo: Esther Kang

ISBN 978-0-8308-4597-2 (print)
ISBN 978-0-8308-4823-2 (digital)

Printed in the United States of America ∞

Library of Congress Cataloging-in-Publication Data
A catalog record for this book is available from the Library of Congress.

P	21	20	19	18	17	16	15	14	13	12	11	10	9	8	7	6	5	4	3	2	1
Y	37	36	35	34	33	32	31	30	29	28	27	26	25	24	23	22	21	20			

To my sons, Eliot and Winston.

This is for you.

And to Maggie,

who is our compass.

TABLE OF CONTENTS

FOREWORD

BY BRENDA SALTER McNEIL

"WE LIKED YOU BETTER when you just quoted Bible verses!"

That's what an angry white Christian man wrote to me one day on social media. His comment stung when I first read it, but then I said to myself, "I bet you did!"

After thinking about it, I believe he posted this comment because I've become much more vocal about exposing white supremacist ideology. For years, I intentionally avoided speaking out about controversial social and political issues because I believed that if I could convince Christian people that reconciliation was biblical, they would embrace it and pursue it. But that didn't happen! Instead, many of the evangelical Christians who invited me to speak at their churches, colleges, and conferences also voted for an American president who degraded and ridiculed women, people of color, immigrants, and people with disabilities. That's when I knew I had to speak out more forcefully about the truth of racial reconciliation, which would require directly confronting the issue of whiteness.

It is deeply disturbing that so many Christians think that racial reconciliation is some kind of liberal, politically motivated social agenda that has nothing to do with their faith as followers of Jesus Christ. It is also an indictment on the church that so many Christians are discipled and don't know that the gospel includes reconciliation across racial, gender, ethnic, social, and cultural barriers. Discipleship is an invitation to follow Jesus into a new community. We are called to make disciples who create corporate, social change as a part of a new community that loves the Lord with all our heart, mind, soul, and strength, and loves our neighbor as ourselves.

Unfortunately, since so many Christians have not heard this message, there is an urgent need for rediscipling in the Christian community.

That's why I'm so excited about this book by David Swanson. David offers a new discipleship pathway by speaking honestly and precisely to white people and elevating the voices and histories of people of color who have been calling for a more honest conversation about faith and race all along. *Rediscipling the White Church* is a unique contribution to this discussion because, unlike other white people who keep denying it, David tells the truth about the reality of whiteness in the church and society. He gives language to what many people of color have experienced and felt about the way whiteness functions. More importantly, however, he also is willing to take the hit himself and not just let people of color withstand the worst of the angry attacks from defensive white Christians.

David knows that racism is insidious, and he has chosen to expose how it operates so we can all see it and be healed of its power and influence over us. I can't think of anybody I trust more to write this important book. I have known David and have been on the journey of life and reconciliation with him for over ten years. I can personally vouch for his credibility as an ally who lives in solidarity with and submission to the black community where he lives, worships, and serves.

In this book, David is intellectually rigorous as he analyzes the current problem and synthesizes solutions with great care and precision. He also knows and firmly believes that we need the power of the Holy Spirit to transform us. That's why he unflinchingly confesses the truth about the wickedness of racism and dismantles whiteness so people can be healed, while also casting a compelling spiritual vision that leads toward the future with hope.

I experienced this firsthand at a conference at New Life Church in Queens, New York, where David was preaching about the Holy Spirit. Although I was also one of the speakers at this event, I was struggling with my hope for reconciliation in a world where so much pain, injustice, deceit, hypocrisy, violence, and divisiveness were taking place.

At the end of David's sermon, he said, "Holy Spirit–empowered rebels will defy this nation's racial oppression with the gospel of reconciliation!" Then he boldly and prophetically declared in a loud voice,

"Racism will die. Oppression will die. White supremacy will die. But you, child of God, will live!"

In that instant, something that felt like a green sprig of hope sprang up out of the barren ground of my soul! It was the first time in a long time that I truly felt a sense of hope about the future of reconciliation in the church.

So I pray that after reading this book you, too, will experience a new sense of hope that God has the power to raise up disciples who are agents of racial healing in a world that so desperately needs to see credible witnesses of the kingdom of God. May it be so!

FROM CHEAP DIVERSITY . . .

"I don't know what to do." "I've never been here before." "This is new for me." "I was caught completely by surprise."

Over the previous few years I've heard many variations of these laments from white pastors and ministry leaders. I've listened as they've reflected on waking up to the presence of some harmful racial assumptions within their communities, assumptions that have been exposed and encouraged by our nation's increasingly divisive political climate.

I remember a Latina friend telling me how her congregation experienced the most recent presidential election. The public rhetoric about immigrants and refugees had instilled fear in her community, and she began crying as she described how her church had fasted and prayed in the days before an important national election. She knew, though, that her story was unlikely to be received in many white churches. Sadly, I think she was right. Experiences like hers are often dismissed when shared in white Christian spaces. Rather than setting aside political commitments to show concern and compassion, all too often white Christians ignore people like my friend.

Stories like this are alerting ministry leaders to the fact that within white Christianity—churches, ministries, and other Christian communities that are racially, demographically, and culturally white—something is wrong. In the pages to come, we'll get more specific about the characteristics of white Christianity and see why, if we are to reflect the gospel's call to reconciliation, it's necessary to address it precisely.

For many white Christians, the failure to prioritize racial justice and reconciliation has become undeniable. They are noticing that great numbers of other white Christians seem to have more in common with those who share their race rather than those who share their faith. As they become aware of their congregations' racial assumptions and blind spots, these pastors and ministry leaders are also viewing their communities' racial sameness with new eyes.

I'm thinking about a recent racial reconciliation retreat I attended, where a white woman described how her black friend had shared vulnerably about the challenges she had experienced in their predominantly white church. Her friend's honesty opened this woman's eyes to some of the harmful biases and divisive assumptions she'd previously missed. I'm also thinking about a friend who pastors a white congregation in a midwestern farming town. This church generously supports a new African American church in a nearby city, and my friend has developed a relationship with the black church planter. Yet as my friend has listened closely to some of the racial assumptions held by members of his own church, he can't help but notice how regularly their assumptions miss the realities faced by their black ministry partners.

Many white Christians across America are waking up to the fact that something is seriously wrong—but often this is where we get stuck. The prospect of addressing racial blind spots and assumptions can seem impossible, especially when the members of our communities are content with the way things are—or, as is often the case in this country, when our neighborhoods and towns appear to offer little in the way of cultural diversity.

For many of these Christians, the response to these blind spots and assumptions has been to become—or at least *try* to become—more racially diverse. But is diversity even the answer to the racial blind spots we're beginning to recognize? Should we pursue racial, ethnic, and cultural diversity as the answer to the racial dysfunctions we are beginning to recognize?[1]

I agree that there is something wrong in white Christianity, though for the past ten years I've lived and done ministry largely outside its bounds. Our church's neighborhood is largely African American, and the congregation itself is racially and ethnically diverse. My own neighborhood is very diverse, as is our children's public elementary school. The pastors and ministry leaders who have mentored our church are almost all women and men of color. I mention these details to point out that for the past decade my vantage point on white Christianity has been one of distance and reflection. My understanding of homogeneously white ministry has changed over these years, aided by the multiracial community to which I belong. From these women and men, I've come to see that the segregation inherent in the Christianity I grew up in is not neutral or merely a reflection of individual choices and preferences.

We don't really talk about segregation anymore. The word sounds like a relic of the civil rights movement, an era to be studied clinically from the distance of history. Most white people, despite the racial homogeneity of most of our churches, don't think of ourselves as being segregated from people of color. And we certainly don't imagine that we actively contribute to the racial segregation of our society.

Consider, though, the racial and ethnic demographics of our churches. As a group, white evangelicals are 76 percent racially homogeneous while mainline Protestant denominations are 86 percent white. Though some denominations are racially diverse, the individual congregations within them are overwhelmingly not. Using a sociological definition, no more than 12 to 14 percent of American congregations are racially mixed.[2]

Typically, Christian organizations that are predominantly white think of their demographics as an accident of personal or cultural preference. Yes, we realize that 11:00 a.m. on a Sunday morning may be the country's most segregated hour, but we have understood this to be a relatively benign segregation. But now, as racial tensions and divisions become increasingly visible, ministry leaders are rethinking the real-world impact of their churches' racial homogeneity.

With all its ugly implications, *segregation* is the right word for what we have long ignored. It's just that now, in the endless culture wars fought on cable news and social media, it's harder to miss how segregation undermines the witness of the body of Christ.

■ ■ ■

Despite my own situation in racially diverse communities and my deep commitment to the multiracial church, my years outside of white Christianity have not led me to think of racial, ethnic, and cultural diversity as the answer to the problem ailing white Christianity. The reason for this is simple: the segregation within white Christianity is not fundamentally a diversity problem: it's a discipleship problem. Addressing white Christianity's lack of diversity without first reckoning with our discipleship would be like redecorating a house built on a failing foundation. Before white churches pursue racial, ethnic, and cultural diversity as the solution to our segregation, we must first address the discipleship that led to our segregation in the first place.

Discipleship is rarely discussed at the intersection of race and Christianity, even though it is central to the identity of every church seeking to be faithful to Jesus' Great Commission in Matthew 28. Could this neglect explain why white Christians are better known for partisanship than reconciled communities across cultural lines of division? These days we seem more committed to culture wars than to proclaiming the gospel of the kingdom of God. The racial isolation that marks white Americans in general is just as pronounced among Christians. And, as has become sadly evident in recent years, our ears are often attuned more to our preferred partisan media sources than to the church of color down the street. Race keeps us from seeing how much we hold in common with our siblings in Christ.

My claim, then, is that in order to address our segregation, white churches and ministries must begin with discipleship, not diversity. In Part One we will explore how American culture disciples white Christians toward racial segregation and injustice. Our imaginations, desires, and assumptions are constantly shaped by historically rooted and socially constructed racial narratives that result in our segregation. Instead of identifying and resisting these false narratives, most of our Christian discipleship practices have ignored them, and in doing so we have told generations of white Christians that Jesus has nothing to say about racial injustice and segregation.

Nearly twenty years ago, sociologists Christian Smith and Michael Emerson identified the characteristics of white Christianity that sabotage our attempts at racial reconciliation. It's important that we understand these characteristics so as to not underestimate how difficult is our task of confronting racial segregation and injustice with reimagined discipleship practices.

Perhaps the most painful part of this journey comes when we honestly assess the damage done by our defective forms of discipleship. Our segregation has weakened our witness to the gospel and inflicted real suffering on members of the Christian family, women and men of color who share our faith in Jesus as Lord and Savior but who have been made all but invisible by our racial blinders.

Confessing our failure to disciple people in the way of Jesus will be difficult. The temptation to pull back, to look for an easier way to address the unease we feel about our churches, will be strong. But there are no quick fixes, no prescribed steps to a racially reconciled church. Instead, our own repentance over shallow spiritual formation and harmful segregation is a prerequisite for the way forward.

But this difficult way of discipleship points to a hopeful horizon. In Part Two, after having reckoned with the extent of our segregation, we will envision discipleship practices that lead white Christians into solidarity with the diverse body of Christ. These chapters are not a comprehensive curriculum, nor are they exhaustive about how to disciple white Christians away from segregation. Instead, we'll take what we observed in the first few chapters and apply that to some essential expressions of Christian ministry.

■ ■ ■

Over the years I've heard countless white Christian leaders express a desire to address racial injustices—leaders whose homogeneous settings make them unsure how to do it. This is why beginning the journey toward solidarity in discipleship is so promising: anyone can do it! Because we aren't starting with racial diversity, what matters most is not whether your ministry, neighborhood, or region is diverse or, as one pastor described his town to me, "lily white." What matters initially is what has always been most important to the church: a commitment to Jesus' command to make disciples, now reimagined to form white Christians away from segregation and into solidarity with the body of Christ. In the spiritual battle for a more reconciled church, every single majority-white congregation has a significant role to play, and it begins with discipleship.

■ ■ ■

By now it might seem that I am writing only to white Christians. This both is and is not true. The problem I'm addressing—segregating discipleship—originates in white churches. White ministry leaders are responsible for addressing this corporate sin and leading their communities closer to the way of Jesus. In this regard I, as a white pastor, am speaking to my people. But because I belong to a racially diverse congregation located in an African American neighborhood, my people are not all white. They're not even mostly white. This means that even though I address this book with love and hope to those serving in majority-white settings, I cannot help but picture friends and ministry colleagues who serve the church outside the bounds of white Christianity.[3] The segregation we'll uncover in the coming pages has real, destructive power in these communities. I've personally observed it in the lives of those I serve. But the solidarity that is available through reimagined discipleship is a power to which I can also personally and joyfully attest.

None of this is theoretical. Our decision to reject the defective discipleship that fosters segregation for reimagined practices that lead us toward solidarity with the body of Christ has real-world impact on countless fellow members of that body. The challenges before us are great; the segregation we have fostered has deep roots. But the possibilities are even greater, and it's this vision of Christians reconciled across racial, ethnic, and cultural divides, bearing brilliant witness to Jesus, that urges us forward.

CHAPTER ONE

DISCIPLED BY RACE

A FEW YEARS AGO I was quietly reading in the living room of our first-floor Chicago apartment. Earlier that day I'd patched a hole in the sidewalk in front of our building and then placed a barricade of yellow tape across it to protect the wet cement. It was a pleasant autumn afternoon, and I'd opened the window, so when someone began loudly tearing down the tape, I could hear it clearly.

In the three seconds it took to run from the couch to the window, an image of the person destroying my work jumped into my mind: a student from the local public high school. If I'm completely honest here, the person who appeared in my imagination was a young black man. Instead, when I reached the window, I saw someone else, a young white guy, likely a student at the prestigious university in our neighborhood. A sense of frustrated entitlement exuded from his stomping, ripping, and angry cursing. You might think that I yelled at him to stop, but instead I was caught short by what had just taken place—not on the sidewalk but in my own imagination. I walked back to the couch feeling ashamed. For no rational reason I had made an assumption about who was ruining my hard work. Even more troubling, if my own two eyes hadn't seen otherwise, I'd still be assigning blame to an innocent black man—a figment of my imagination—to this day.

Social scientists describe moments like these as evidence of unconscious bias—assumptions existing beyond our awareness that we hold about groups of people. There are online tests that show the implicit bias most Americans have (for example, against African Americans), but on that autumn afternoon I didn't need an online test to prove my prejudice.[1] I had just failed my own, real-life version of an implicit bias test.

I'm not alone in my failure. By almost every measure, American society demonstrates racial biases that center certain people within it—white men like myself, for example—while marginalizing others. Everything from access to credit, accumulating generational wealth, engaging with law enforcement, treatment by health care professionals, and even the likelihood of a mother's death while giving birth are affected by our collective racial biases against people of color, and especially African Americans and Native Americans.[2]

We don't leave these biases behind at the entrances of our churches. White Christianity is deeply susceptible to and complicit in the racial biases that inflict damage on people of color. As my own story shows, it's not that most of us are consciously choosing these racial biases; they've simply attached themselves to our imaginations and assumptions. It's our task in this chapter to understand how this happens.

To do this we will examine the racial segregation within white Christianity through the lens of discipleship. There are two important reasons to do this. First, discipleship is central to Christianity. As philosopher Dallas Willard put it, "The New Testament is a book about disciples, by disciples, and for disciples of Jesus Christ."[3] Any discussion about a change in a Christian's beliefs or behaviors—including those related to racial justice and reconciliation—must begin with our discipleship to Jesus.

The second, perhaps less obvious, reason that discipleship is critical for addressing racial injustice and segregation is that discipleship is not limited to Christianity. There is another kind of discipleship at work on us, and it has been mostly invisible to white Christians. If white Christians are ever to move past the cultural lines of segregation, we'll need to understand this other discipleship. Only then can we reimagine Christian practices that will form us away from the destructive segregation of our culture and into solidarity with the racially, ethnically, and culturally diverse body of Christ.

So let's take a look at these two discipleships: Christian discipleship that nurtures solidarity across cultural lines of division and the racial discipleship that builds walls of segregation and fosters racial injustice.

■ ■ ■

The word *disciple* occurs close to three hundred times in the New Testament. Yet despite how often it's used, discipleship can be a fuzzy concept. Jesus commanded his followers to make disciples in some of his final instructions before his ascension (Matthew 28:16-20), so we know it's a priority. But as Christians, inheritors of Jesus' command to make disciples, what do we actually mean by discipleship? Because we will rely so thoroughly on discipleship both to understand what is wrong within white Christianity as well as to imagine a hopeful way forward, it's important to be precise. To do this there are two important questions to answer: What is a disciple? and, How are disciples made? Let's begin with the first.

In his classic book about discipleship and the kingdom of God, *The Divine Conspiracy*, Dallas Willard claims that a disciple is, most basically, an apprentice "who has decided to be with another person, under appropriate conditions, in order to become capable of doing what that person does or to become what that person is."[4] This will become clearer when we turn to racial discipleship, but it's important to notice that there is nothing uniquely Christian about discipleship. Basically, we're thinking about the relationship between a student and her teacher in which the student follows the teacher to become like her teacher in order to do what the teacher does.

The teacher-disciple relationship is different than the education many of us have received. The educational goal for most of us was the transfer of knowledge from one person to another. But the teacher-disciple relationship is just that: a relationship, through which the student takes on the character of the teacher in order to enact the teacher's authority.

While this "follow-become-do" relationship between a teacher and disciple is not inherently Christian, it's easy to see how it became the defining relationship between Jesus and his followers. Remember, for example, how Jesus called his first disciples to *follow* him, as with Peter and his brother James as they were fishing (Mark 1:17). Or think about Jesus' assumption in Luke 6:40 that disciples *become* like their teachers: "The student is not above the teacher, but everyone who is fully trained will be like their teacher." It's an expectation that Paul makes explicit in 2 Corinthians 3:18: "And we all, who with unveiled faces contemplate the Lord's glory, are being transformed into his image with ever-increasing glory, which comes from the Lord, who is the Spirit." Finally, Jesus expects that his disciples will *do* what they have seen him do. When Jesus appointed his twelve apostles in Mark 3:14-15, he did so that "they might be with him and that he might send them out to preach and to have authority to drive out demons." Just three chapters later, Jesus kept his word, sending the disciples with his authority to do what they had seen him do. So Christian discipleship is not simply obeying what Jesus said; it's also learning to do what he did.

While there is more that could be said about what a disciple is, for our purposes a Christian disciple follows Jesus to become like him and to do what he does.

■ ■ ■

We can now turn to our second question: How are disciples made?

When thinking about making disciples, we often begin with what Christians believe and then consider how those beliefs are lived out. American ministry often displays the conviction that the process of discipleship is believing new things about God and then acting on those beliefs. So, for example, Jesus taught that the most important commandments are to love God and love our neighbor as ourselves. We think that knowing this—*really* believing it—is what is necessary for Christians to follow Jesus' example, to love our neighbors as much as we love ourselves.

But this understanding of discipleship—in which correct thinking or believing leads to Christlike actions—significantly misunderstands the basic nature of our humanity. It assumes that we move through the world directed mostly by our minds, as rational beings who think our way toward the good and away from what is sinful. But as Saint Augustine

knew, humans are not mostly thinking or believing beings: we are creatures of desire whose loves orient us through the world. In *Confessions*,
this fifth-century North African bishop cautioned against the many
things we find alluring in this world: "For they go their way and are no
more; and they rend the soul with desire that can destroy it, for it longs
to be one with the things it loves and to repose in them. But in them is
no place to repose, because they do not abide."[5] As Augustine writes
earlier, it isn't that the ends to which our desires orient us are not "things
of beauty." Rather, he's pointing out that as desiring beings it is our nature
to find ultimate meaning in what we most love, famously expressing at
the beginning of his *Confessions*, "Thou hast made us for Thyself and our
hearts are restless till they rest in Thee."[6]

A discussion of this ancient bishop's anthropology may seem a long
way from our immediate concern about racial justice and reconciliation
within white Christianity. But because our lens is discipleship, it's essential that we consider how people are formed in real life. Jesus did not
come to present us with a new set of doctrines or to correct some faulty
thinking. As important as right belief is—and it is!—Jesus made it plain
that he came to transform us at the deepest possible level, "For the
mouth speaks what the heart is full of" (Luke 6:45). Addressing what is
wrong within white Christianity must begin with our desires and loves.

Think back to our definition of a Christian disciple: following Jesus
to become like Jesus, in order to do what Jesus does. It is in the *becoming*
that Augustine's insights prove so important. Grasping that we are desiring beings allows us to see how we become more like Jesus. So, how
are our desires shaped to reflect those of our Savior?

■ ■ ■

Building on Augustine's understanding of people as desiring creatures, philosopher James K. A. Smith writes that it's our *habits* that
"incline us to act in certain ways without having to kick into a mode of
reflection."[7] Remember my implicit bias at the beginning of the
chapter? Because we are not first and foremost thinking beings who
rationally engage with every encounter, it is our habits which shape our
imaginations or, in Augustine's vocabulary, our loves. My unconscious

assumption about who wrecked my cement was inculcated in me through a set of racially oriented habits.

We aren't usually aware of our habits. In fact, we mostly don't have the time or capacity to think about how they constantly direct our desires. Smith gives the example of a commuter whose daily habits allow her to make the drive without consciously thinking through each step of navigation required to get her car from home to work and then back again. More than once, walking from my car into our apartment, I've realized that I can't remember the drive home. It's a scary thought, but this is how our habits are supposed to work. (If you're ever riding with me, I promise I'll think about driving safely!)

A more difficult example of how habits direct our desires and assumptions is the implicit bias that surfaced when my wet cement got wrecked. In the split second between hearing the wreckage and forming the assumption, I didn't have time to rationally think things through. Rather, a set of racially oriented habits had already been at work deep within me to shape how I imagined the world, including what kind of person would intentionally step into my cement.

■ ■ ■

Understanding people as desiring beings whose assumptions are aimed by unconscious habits gets us closer to understanding how disciples are made and why discipleship is the way to address racial segregation within white Christianity. But there are a couple more aspects of our humanity that we need to include. It's one thing to say that our desires are directed by our habits, but how are these habits formed? Again, we are considering the *becoming* aspect of our definition of a Christian disciple. As flesh-and-blood creatures who move through the world guided by our desires, what forms the habits that in turn orient our desires?

Here again, Smith is helpful. It is communal *practices* that shape our habits, "routines and rituals that inscribe particular ongoing habits into our character, such that they become second nature to us."[8] Whether or not we intentionally choose to engage in a particular practice, the results are the same. Over time these practices form habits that then aim our desires. Practices, writes Smith, are never neutral. So we must ask, "Just what kind of person is this habit or practice trying to produce, and to what end is such a practice aimed?"[9] In other words, if we want to understand why I, as a desiring being, leapt to certain assumptions about the person who destroyed my wet cement, we need to trace those assumptions through my habits and to the biased practices that shaped them.

In the gospels of Matthew and Mark, Jesus began his ministry with a simple proclamation: "The kingdom of God/heaven has come near" (Mark 1:15 and Matthew 3:2). The rest of the gospel accounts can be read as Jesus' mission to announce this kingdom and to demonstrate its power. His atoning and victorious death and resurrection inaugurated this kingdom into which we invite new disciples to this very day. Congruent with our view of people as desiring beings, Jesus does not announce this kingdom through a new list of doctrines, though he does plenty of teaching. Rather, his disciples are exposed to mystifying parables, displays of power, and, most importantly, the person of Jesus himself in all sorts of circumstances: weddings, funerals, storms, long journeys, and uncomfortable cross-cultural encounters.

Yet despite Jesus' intentionality with his disciples, the kingdom of God eluded their imaginations. For example, Jesus tells his followers that the last will be first in the kingdom, but the disciples keep arguing about who among them is the greatest. Another time the disciples worry about forgetting the bread for one of their road trips right after Jesus had miraculously fed thousands! Their most consistent misunderstanding came whenever Jesus explained that the kingdom of God would come through his death. This vision of God's will was so beyond the disciples' imaginations that they simply couldn't reconcile it with their views of the world.

Of course, the kingdom of God has often eluded our own imaginations. A Native American friend told me that even the word *kingdom* carries too much terrible history for her. As a Christian she realizes the significance of this biblical word, yet the way it is so deeply connected with the European colonization that resulted in the genocide of her ancestors has proven a significant challenge, and she continues to wrestle with it. The ways we have forced God's righteous and peaceful rule into our violent and exploitative agendas shows how often our own imaginations have failed us.

In announcing the kingdom of God, Jesus was inviting his disciples into what philosopher Charles Taylor calls a new "social imaginary." Rather than thinking about a worldview shaped by Christian beliefs, understanding people as desiring beings is better served by highlighting the importance of our imaginations. A social imaginary is "the way ordinary people 'imagine' their social surroundings, and this is often not expressed in theoretical terms, it is carried in images, satires, legends, etc."[10] The way you and I experience the world, and what we expect from it, largely results from how we *imagine* the world. For the disciples this meant navigating through the world as occupied Jewish people who longed for God's messiah to rescue them from their Roman oppressors. No wonder the kingdom of God was so hard for them to grasp. It was, to a large extent, beyond their capacity to imagine!

Our desires are not static. They point to our ultimate love. As Christians who worship King Jesus, our desires are meant to orient us toward his kingdom. Yet like Jesus' first disciples, the way we imagine the world at the deepest level of our being is often at odds with the kingdom Jesus announced and inaugurated. So any vision for making Christian disciples must account for the kingdom of God as well as those competing kingdoms that disorder and disorient our desires. Otherwise, like Jesus' first disciples, we'll be confused or we'll even reject the very kingdom Jesus came to announce. And as we'll see, racial discipleship is sustained by a social imaginary directly opposed to the kingdom of God.

To our initial definition of Christian discipleship as following Jesus to become like Jesus in order to do what Jesus does, we have now added the elements of humans as desiring beings (whose desires are aimed by habit-shaping practices) who move imaginatively through the world. Making disciples, then, is about inviting people into intentional communal practices that both reflect and announce the kingdom of God. These habit-shaping practices orient our desires and, thus, our actions toward the kingdom and its King. This view of disciple-making resonates with St. Augustine's stirring conviction: "The whole life of a good Christian is an holy desire."[11]

Christian disciples are made, then, as they *follow Jesus (into the kingdom of God) to become like Jesus (through habit-shaping practices that orient their desires) in order to do what Jesus does.* In the second part of the book, we'll focus on the second set of parentheses, to reimagine Christian practices that disciple white Christians away from segregation and into solidarity with the body of Christ. But for now, with this definition in mind, we face a difficult question related to the first set of parentheses: Is white Christianity making disciples whose desires are oriented toward the kingdom of God?

■ ■ ■

While the Bible doesn't address race or racial segregation, it does have plenty to say about the gospel's impact on the sorts of cultural and ethnic divisions and hierarchies that have become racialized in our American context. Paul repeatedly explains how Jesus' death was the means to reconcile people to God as well as to one another. In Christ, the apostle Paul claims in Ephesians 2:14-18, God has made a new humanity from those who had previously lived as enemies.

If the very center of Christian faith—the crucifixion of Jesus—proclaims reconciliation across cultural divisions, then so much of what we find in the New Testament flows naturally: Jesus prays for our unity (John 17:20-21); the Holy Spirit grants the gift of tongues at Pentecost that the gospel might be proclaimed to the multilingual nations (Acts 2:1-12); Philip is sent to baptize the Ethiopian eunuch (Acts 8:26-40); Peter is sent to eat with Cornelius, the Roman centurion (Acts 10); and, by the thirteenth chapter of Acts, we find the first multicultural church, pastored by diverse leaders who were reconciled by the gospel (Acts 13:1). These early disciples had been formed toward a vision of the kingdom of God that was experienced as a new family comprised of former cultural enemies.

Can the same be said of white Christianity? The answer, I'm afraid, is no. A 2013 survey by the Public Religion Research Institute found that the social networks of white Americans are 91 percent white and that "fully three-quarters (75 percent) of whites have entirely white social networks without any minority presence."[12] Most white people, in other words, have no people of color within the social networks that make up their lives. No other racial group exhibits this level of segregation; as the cultural majority, it's only white Americans who have the option to not interact cross-culturally on a regular basis.

But, we might protest, this segregation is true of all white Americans, not just Christians. That's true, but when we look within white Christianity for contemporary evidence of the early church's reconciliation, the picture is bleak. White evangelical Protestants support political movements to ban or severely restrict refugees at rates higher than almost every other demographic. More than any other religious group, white evangelicals believe that increasing cultural diversity in the United States is a negative development—this despite the fact that the majority of new immigrants are Christians. Consider also the segregation within white churches that we noted in the introduction.[13]

My point isn't to beat up on white Christianity. As noted earlier, the biases and assumptions that lead to the disheartening realities in the previous paragraph are in many ways simply the air we breathe, the world as we've been formed to imagine it. Even so, we must be honest about the problem many of us have sensed because it is deadly serious. For the most part, white Christianity is not making disciples who reflect and announce the division-healing kingdom of God, and the evidence is plain to see. And the reason for this failure of discipleship is profound if also relatively simple. White Christianity has been blind to the powerful racial discipleship that has formed the imaginations of white Christians. And it's to this insidious discipleship that we must now turn.

■ ■ ■

If the kingdom of God is one in which racial, ethnic, and cultural divides are reconciled by Jesus' atoning and victorious death and resurrection, the social imaginary of the United States is powerfully corrupted by what author and the founder of the Equal Justice Initiative, Bryan Stevenson, calls "the narrative of racial difference." For Stevenson, whose work links chattel slavery, lynching, and contemporary mass incarceration, the critical component that our analysis of racial injustice often overlooks is a set of assumptions that dehumanizes entire groups of people. How we imagine the world has been infected by this narrative of racial difference.

In an interview, Stevenson described how the narrative of racial difference came to dominate the American imagination.

> You can't understand many of the most destructive issues or policies in our country without understanding our history of racial inequality. And I actually think it begins with our interaction with native people, because we took land, we killed people, we disrupted a culture. We were brutal. And we justified and rationalized that land grab, that genocide, by characterizing native people as different. It was the first way in which this narrative of racial difference was employed to justify behaviors that would otherwise be unjustifiable. When you are allowed to demonize another community and call them savages, and treat them brutally and cruelly, it changes your psyche. We abused and mistreated the communities and cultures that existed on this land before Europeans arrived, and then that narrative of racial difference was used to develop slavery. . . . I genuinely believe that, despite all of that victimization, the worst part of slavery was this narrative that we created about black people—this idea that black people aren't fully human, that they are three-fifths human, that they are not capable, that they are not evolved. That ideology, which set up white supremacy in America, was the most poisonous and destructive consequence of two centuries of slavery. And I do believe that we never addressed it.[14]

This narrative is not one that white Americans typically discuss or even acknowledge. In fact, most of us are happy to publicly affirm racial equality. Yet the lived realities of Americans of different races point to how this narrative is alive and well, even in an era in which almost everyone purports to believe in racial justice. We can think of the narrative of racial difference as invisibly polluted air or contaminated water; the fact that we don't recognize it doesn't dull its impact on our way of moving through the world.

In contrast to a vision of the kingdom of God, the narrative of racial difference shapes our imaginations toward racial segregation and injustice. To make matters worse, our habit-oriented desires are constantly being shaped by cultural practices that reinforce this warped vision of the world and our neighbors. In a society whose imagination has been infected by the narrative of racial difference, we should expect that our communal practices are forming racial habits that in turn deform our assumptions about racial justice and reconciliation.

As professor Eddie Glaude writes, our racial habits are "the ways we live the belief that white people are valued more than others. They are the things we do, without thinking, that sustain the value gap. They range from the snap judgments we make about black people that rely on stereotypes to the ways we think about race that we get from living within our respective communities."[15] They are so deeply embedded within American society that they have become instinctual, a product of our racially dysfunctional imaginations. Our racial habits are formed not through an understanding of complex and racially unjust practices, but by the observable outcomes produced by those practices.

Racial habits, Glaude continues, are learned "not by way of overt racism but through the details of daily life, like when we experience the differences in the quality of the schools we attend, the different nature of our interactions with the police, the different ways we navigate where we work, our different neighborhoods, and the daily barrage of signals and cues about race that all Americans get through television and news reports."[16] It is practices like these—the education system, law enforcement, employment, and housing, among others—that form the racial habits that in turn direct our desires away from the reconciled kingdom of God.

When it comes to racial injustice, most of us aren't thinking about this sort of discipleship. Rather, white Christians tend to think individualistically about race, imagining both injustice and reconciliation as natural products of our relational choices. To better understand how our assumptions have been formed by racial habits that, in turn, have been shaped by practices infected by the narrative of racial difference, let's consider briefly just one of these examples: where we live.

Maybe the choice of where to live doesn't seem like a racial practice, but it's that very hiddenness that often characterizes how social practices function. While some of our habits are practiced intentionally, just as many are being formed without our knowledge by societal practices that seem so normal, they're all but invisible. By not noticing how these practices are shaping us, we fail to account for the kinds of people they are forming us to be. So, how does where we live function in this desire-orienting way?

While we often think of where we live as a matter of personal preference, there is actually a massive amount of policy and legislation behind where we reside. As historian Richard Rothstein shows in *The Color of Law*, because racial discrimination was official federal policy through the middle of the twentieth century, black citizens were excluded from federally insured mortgages.[17] Not only that, housing developers were only eligible for government insurance if they maintained a strict policy of banning African Americans from inhabiting the homes they built. The racial divide we see today between many affluent suburbs and nearby urban neighborhoods is not an accident of history nor the amalgamation of countless individual choices; it is *de jure* (according to law) segregation, constructed and sustained by federal and, in many cases, state and local government policies.

This means that the majority of us live where we do not simply as a matter of preference or convenience. How we decide where to live is shaped by what we might call a housing practice. This practice, like all our racial practices, is infected with the narrative of racial difference, which maps each American citizen onto a racial hierarchy. The impact of *de jure* segregation is so significant that race has become an accurate predictor of whether someone's neighborhood is impoverished or proximate to hazardous waste facilities. Also, because home equity is the major source of wealth in America, the descendants of black people who couldn't access federally backed mortgages generations ago now hold only a fraction of the wealth of the average white person.

Each of us exists within this swirl of racially determined decisions and outcomes when it comes to where we live. We're simply unaware of it most of the time. So this racial practice—the practice of choosing a home and neighborhood, as well as the myriad of daily habits that are formed by it—slowly and subtly directs our desires and assumptions. We are being oriented not toward the kingdom of God but to a different, racially unjust and segregated one. The narrative of racial difference is strengthened in our imagination as we send our children off to local schools where "good" means white and "struggling," "underperforming," or some other euphemism means that the children come from the black or brown parts of town.

I still remember a phone call I received ten years ago. A white friend from the suburb where my wife and I had previously lived wanted to visit us in our new, urban neighborhood. But because our apartment was in a majority-black region of the city, he wanted to make sure that he could drive home safely before it got dark. No matter that our neighborhood is one of the most policed in the city or that, as a white man, there is nowhere he could go in the city and not be relatively safe. His imagination, in large part formed by the mostly white suburb where he lived, shaped his understanding of reality. Like my wrong assumptions about who stomped through my wet cement, this friend was acting out an imagination that had been oriented through a set of racial practices. At least one of those practices had to do with where he lived.

We could also look at other examples of racial practices—the education system, law enforcement, and employment—and find similar desire-orienting dynamics at work. Racial discipleship is framed by the narrative of racial difference and formed by racial practices. As desiring beings, our imaginations and desires are constantly being oriented away from division-healing solidarity with the body of Christ and into the racial segregation that has always characterized this country and its churches. Because white Christianity has largely ignored this deforming cultural discipleship, we have been unable to resist it. Instead, we leave our people to its isolating and concealing power, content to explain away our racial, ethnic, and cultural isolation as anything other than complicity with a system so totally opposed to the kingdom of God.

■ ■ ■

It can be painful to acknowledge how inept white Christianity has been at confronting the destructive narrative of racial difference and the racial practices that shape our habits. The churches and ministries of my own childhood and youth, full of men and women who loved Jesus and mentored me faithfully, fall squarely within this racially homogeneous version of Christianity. Part of me feels like I'm betraying those I love or exposing shameful family secrets. The pain that comes with assessing the failure to expose and resist racial discipleship can cause some of us to turn back or give up. But I have found that painful honesty leads to hope. This is because, despite the depth of our failure, habits can be reshaped, including the racial ones so deeply ingrained in us. And, as we'll explore in Part Two, ancient Christian practices, empowered by the Holy Spirit, can be reimagined to seriously reckon with the deceptive narrative of racial difference and its accompanying segregating practices.

My desires and assumptions had already been deeply and subtly formed before my imagination betrayed me over some wet cement that autumn afternoon a few years ago. But the fact that my bias against young African American men was revealed in that moment does not leave me forever abandoned to those deformed assumptions. As a disciple of Jesus, my hope is in the one who promised me a new heart and new desires and loves that orient me to the kingdom of God.

CHAPTER TWO

CONCEALED BY RACE

THE *NEW YORK TIMES* REPORTER on the other end of the line sounded genuinely perplexed. He was working on a story about multiracial churches after the 2016 presidential election. Given how racially charged this moment was, how were multiracial churches like ours able to maintain any kind of harmony?

In his interviews with people of color in multiracial congregations, he had found that many of them were struggling to remain in their churches. Some had made the difficult decision to leave for the security and familiarity of an ethnically homogenous congregation. Others had stopped attending church altogether. Many of these Christians had originally been attracted to multiracial churches for the chance to experience more of the cultural diversity of the kingdom of God. Others believed these ministries could make a dent in the country's legacy of racial injustice. Yet as instances of visible racial injustice seemed to increase in recent years, these people of color often experienced a deafening silence from the white people in their churches, including their pastors. One of the women featured in the article described the 2012 killing of Trayvon Martin, a black teenager, as her turning point. About her fellow white congregants she said, "It's not even on your radar and I can't sleep over it. And now that I'm being vocal, you think I've changed."[1] She eventually left the church, feeling as though her fellow members and church leadership would never seriously address her experiences with racial injustice.

As I described to the reporter how our congregation was imperfectly navigating these treacherous waters, I thought about how difficult it has been for white Christians to meaningfully engage with the experiences of our racially diverse family in Christ. Even now, generations removed from legally enforced segregation, white Christians struggle to enter into the experiences of people of color. More than once I've observed a white Christian debate or discount fellow Christians' stories about their experience of racism. Because these difficult testimonies don't match our experiences, we assume they can't be true.

There is nothing new about this dynamic; James Baldwin wrote about it during a trip through the Jim Crow South in 1961: "I was told, several times, by white people, that 'race relations' there were excellent. I failed to find a single Negro who agreed with this, which is the usual story of 'race relations' in this country."[2]

It's not that some white Christians haven't tried to bridge this gap of experience and trust. Sociologists define a multiracial church as one in which no one racial group makes up more than 80 percent of the congregation. Between 1998 and 2012, Protestant churches saw these diverse congregations rise from 3 percent to 12 percent.[3] Yet, as my conversation with the *Times* reporter reveals, statistics don't tell the full story of white Christianity's segregation from the rest of the body of Christ. In fact, sociologists have found that many multiracial churches with a significant percentage of white people end up perpetuating white cultural assumptions. As Dr. Michael Emerson, a leading scholar of multiracial churches, put it, "Currently, in the aggregate, multiracial congregations are doing exactly what pastors of color tell me they fear— that they will serve merely as a tool into white assimilation."[4] So, while the percentage of multiracial congregations has risen, many of these ministries have not confronted the sinful and destructive roots of racial segregation and injustice.

■ ■ ■

While I truly hope that more white ministries become racially and ethnically diverse—after all, it's a vision I've given my life to!—we've already seen why it's important to begin the journey not with diversity but with discipleship. By ignoring how white people's racial habits have been shaped by the racial practices of a nation deceived by the narrative of racial difference, white Christianity has failed to disciple men and women into the kingdom of God.

But ignorance is not the only thing that hinders our attempts at racial reconciliation and justice. In fact, within white Christianity itself are some deeply held assumptions that, however unintentionally, perpetuate racial segregation and injustice. And these assumptions serve to conceal from us the extent of that racial segregation and injustice. So white Christians are often left oblivious—like the people Baldwin encountered during his travels through the South, they're unable to see what people of color cannot afford *not* to see.

This is a disheartening story to tell, but it's one we must grapple with if we are to effectively reimagine discipleship practices that will shape our desire-orienting habits toward solidarity with the body of Christ. In effect, white people are, to quote James Baldwin again, "still trapped in a history which they do not understand; and until they understand it, they cannot be released from it."[5] Then let's try to understand.

■ ■ ■

In the previous chapter we saw how we navigate the world not through conscious, rational decisions but through our imaginations: we mostly intuit the world through the assumptions and narratives we hold about it. For Americans, this intuition is shaped in large part by the narrative of racial difference. In countless ways, how we navigate through life is molded by the unacknowledged messages we receive every day. Because we do not live in a neutral society but one that assigns privilege and inferiority based on race, the messages we internalize are not neutral either.

Here's a relatively benign example. I'm writing this chapter in a coffee shop near our apartment. This particular coffee shop sits on the campus of a major university, and the patrons are mostly undergraduate and graduate students, predominantly white and Asian with a few African Americans and Latinos and Latinas; it's an accurate representation of the diversity of the university and the neighborhood as a whole. Behind the counter, though, it's a different story. Every employee in this service-sector business is black.

On the surface there's nothing wrong about the racial demographics of this coffee shop's patrons and employees. However, because we breathe the smog of our society's narrative of racial difference and because we have been formed by racial discipleship, we are prone to assume that these demographics are natural. We aren't likely to question why it is that in many similar cafes and restaurants around the city, the racial breakdown between highly educated, privileged patrons and service-sector employees will look just like it does in this one. Rather, on a level we're not typically conscious of, we add this experience to a host of others that confirm the narrative of racial difference. Rather than thinking critically through the societal factors that make sense of who serves and who is being served—the acquisition of generational wealth, access to quality childhood education, race-based housing, employment discrimination, and so on—our assumptions are prone to conform to myths based on our society's racial hierarchy.

Maybe the stakes in the coffee shop don't seem so high, but now consider how this racial discipleship infiltrates housing policies, public education systems, policing practices, and other areas. The racial habits that orient our imaginations have a powerful impact on the minds and hearts of white people like me and on the lives of the black baristas who made my cup of coffee.

■ ■ ■

In their influential book, *Divided by Faith: Evangelical Religion and the Problem of Race in America*, sociologists Michael Emerson and Christian Smith identify the dynamic I'm describing as one result of our "racialized society." By this they mean "a society wherein race matters profoundly for differences in life experiences, life opportunities, and social relationships. A racialized society can also be said to be 'a society that allocates differential economic, political, social, and even psychological rewards to groups along racial lines; lines that are socially constructed.'"[6]

Understanding how our society is racialized helps explain why white Christianity has generally failed to resist racial segregation and injustice.

White Americans typically conceptualize racism as located within an obviously racist person—a member of the Ku Klux Klan or a torch-wielding white nationalist—or it is a specific, unfortunate decision, such as when a celebrity or well-known athlete gets caught saying something racist. In other words, we think about racial injustice in individual terms: a particular person or choice. But while racial discipleship certainly affects individuals and choices, it is much larger than any one individual. It's an entire set of cultural practices that are always working to shape our habits and turn us away from the reconciled kingdom of God. It's not that conscious, racially biased decisions don't matter, but that even seemingly benign, unconscious choices can contribute to segregation and injustice within a racialized society. To adequately disciple white Christians away from racial segregation and injustice, our discipleship practices need to account for racism beyond individual people and decisions. This is exactly what white Christianity has failed to do.

■ ■ ■

To understand why white Christians struggle to engage racial injustice as a system impacting all of society, Emerson and Smith identify three tools that white evangelical Christians use to organize and assess our experiences: freewill individualism, relationalism, and antistructuralism.[7] Because the discipleship practices we will explore in Part Two rely on an understanding of racial injustice that aligns with our racialized society, it's important that we understand these three tools and how they have hindered white Christians' attempts at racial justice and reconciliation.

It's not only white evangelicals who succumb to the discipleship of our racialized society. Most mainline denominations have intentionally pursued racial diversity for decades, yet the scholar Jennifer Harvey notes that segregation remains the norm in these congregations. So, if "the premise of diversity is that difference is to be celebrated and embraced, separate worship must mean we are still resistant to difference somehow and hold negative views of those whose racial identities are distinct from our own."[8] Thus, while there are important differences between white Christianity's conservative and progressive approaches to racial reconciliation, both have failed to genuinely resist the sources of segregation and injustice.

Freewill individualists display a type of American individualism that downplays the importance of institutions while raising the importance of personal accountability. For freewill individualists, people are free to make decisions for themselves that they as individuals will then be accountable for.

Over the years I've listened as many well-meaning white Christians have acknowledged the tragedy of slavery. Some are also aware of the racially oppressive Jim Crow laws and the horrors of lynching in the years following the Civil War. Occasionally these conversation partners can even discuss the rise of mass incarceration and the horrible racial inequities this development represents. Yet even with all of this knowledge, when it comes to responding to racial injustices, these white Christians almost exclusively appeal to the need for personal responsibility and hard work. Yes, they'll acknowledge, horribly unjust things occurred in the past—and continue to this day—and what that requires is for individuals to work that much harder. As inadequate as these responses are, they make complete sense when individualism is the tool of choice for confronting racial injustice.

Relationalism is the next tool preferred by white Christians. It makes sense that a theological movement that prioritizes the restoration of a person's individual relationship with God would highly value interpersonal relationships. Extending this emphasis beyond personal salvation, these Christians believe that social problems are simply a reflection of broken relationships. Solutions to racial inequity are not viewed systemically because, from this vantage point, the root of the problem lies at the relational level. When white Christianity pursues racial justice and reconciliation, relationships between white people and people of color are the priority. White Christianity is willing to acknowledge that racism has kept people apart, but its focus on personal relationships makes it almost impossible to see the systemic nature of our racialized society. So Christians of color who are drawn to multiracial churches often are disappointed when they realize that, for most of the white members, their presence alone indicates success. Meanwhile, the same racial injustices long suffered by people of color continue unabated and, apparently, remain invisible to white Christians.

The last tool used by white Christians is *antistructuralism*. By prioritizing interpersonal relationships as the way to address racial injustice, any focus on unjust social structures is viewed as shifting guilt from the actual source, the individual. As theologian Drew G. I. Hart points out, "Many white people assume racism is only about individual racial prejudice and hatred, and therefore they are always on the lookout for the 'bad racists' to scapegoat."[9] This means that white Christians are often skeptical of the language of social justice, fearing that any attempt to address injustice via *systemic* change is a threat to their *personal* faith.

Taken together, these assumptions, or tools, have made resisting racial segregation and injustice all but impossible for white churches. In fact, as Emerson and Smith soberly note, the tools these churches use to navigate this racialized society ensures that we don't *see* how our society is racialized. And, because "reality is socially constructed, a highly effective way to ensure the perpetuation of a racialized system is simply to deny its existence."[10] When white Christianity has attempted to affect change on racial segregation and injustice, our own deeply held assumptions have undermined our best strategies and models. So rather than knocking down the racial barriers that trouble us, we unwittingly end up reinforcing them.

■ ■ ■

On a tree-lined boulevard in our church's neighborhood sits an old house, unremarkable except for a weathered historical placard standing near the curb to tell passersby that this was Ida B. Wells's home. Wells was born into slavery in Mississippi before becoming a journalist and the nation's leading anti-lynching crusader. For her efforts she was repeatedly threatened and had to flee the South for the relative safety of Chicago.

During an era when hundreds of black men and women were savagely lynched by white mobs, Wells remained steadfast, seemingly fearless in the face of dehumanizing terror. After some of her friends were lynched in Memphis in 1892, Wells took to her newspaper and wrote, "Nobody in this section of the country believes the old thread bare lie that Negro men rape White women. If Southern White men are not careful, they will over-reach themselves and public sentiment will have a reaction; a conclusion will then be reached which will be very damaging to the moral reputation of their women."[11] During a time of overt white terrorism, Well's editorial, truthful as it was, made her a primary target of violence and slander.

In the foreword to one of her books, Wells's close friend, the former slave and abolitionist Frederick Douglass, wrote,

> Brave woman! you have done your people and mine a service which can neither be weighed nor measured. If American conscience were only half alive, if the American church and clergy were only half christianized, if American moral sensibility were not hardened by persistent infliction of outrage and crime against colored people, a scream of horror, shame and indignation would rise to Heaven wherever your pamphlet shall be read.[12]

But no scream of horror rose, especially not from the white churches that Douglass so pointedly indicted. Though many anti-lynching bills were proposed during Wells's lifetime, not a single one was brought to a vote in the Senate.

To read Wells's many accounts of lynchings is to encounter the depths of human depravity. The terror and torture inflicted by white citizens upon their African American neighbors is terrible in the extreme. Bodies were dragged, hung, castrated, and decapitated. Bits of bone and flesh were collected and passed around as souvenirs. Photos of lynched victims were turned into postcards; some were used to advertise upcoming lynchings. I've read these terrible stories and wondered how it was that such public evil could be ignored or tacitly approved of by the majority of white Christians during that era.

Wells must have wondered the same thing. The courageous journalist and outspoken activist was herself the sort of Christian whose language about faith would be at home in most white Christian churches today. For example, after a New Year's Eve worship service in 1886, the twenty-four-year-old returned home and recorded her hopes for the coming year. She wrote, "I go forth on the renewed pilgrimage of this New Year with renewed hope, vigor, a remembrance of the glorious beginnings and humbly pray for wisdom, humility, success in my undertakings if it be My Father's good pleasure, and a stronger Christianity that will make itself felt."[13]

The Chicago to which Wells moved was also home to the ministries of the renowned evangelist Dwight L. Moody. A Bible school and church were among the visible legacies of his ministry, and his reputation was known around the world. Because of Moody's international ministry, when Wells traveled to England to promote her anti-lynching cause, she was asked about the famous pastor. "[The] question was asked what the great moral reformers like . . . Mr. Moody had done to suppress Lynch Law and again I answered—nothing. That Mr. Moody had never said a word against lynching in any of his trips to the South, or in the North either, so far as was known."[14] Like her friend Frederick Douglass, if Wells looked to white Christians for support in the life-and-death battle for racial justice she was almost always met with indifference or opposition. She would find herself alone in advocating for the structural change that sought to spare the lives of innocent black citizens around the country.

I've thought about these two towering giants over the years, citizens of the same country, neighbors in the same city, followers of the same Lord Jesus. Yet the worlds they inhabited were profoundly different, and not just in the obvious ways. While Wells's Christian faith compelled her to think about societal sin and systemic injustice and to respond accordingly, for Moody the focus was squarely on the individual's salvation. This isn't to say the evangelist was completely oblivious to social concerns; his ministry began through an outreach to poor, uneducated youth. But despite the well-known scourge of lynchings, Moody, like most of his white Christian contemporaries, looked away. In this regard, the very different paths taken by Wells and Moody reveal the destructive distance that results from white Christianity's toolbox. Individualism, relationalism, and antistructuralism have built renowned and racially homogenous ministries, but these have been cold comfort to those members of the body of Christ who exist outside the boundaries of racial whiteness.

If white Christians are to reckon with racial discipleship, we must also look critically at the deeply held assumptions that have thus far hindered our attempts to address racial segregation and injustice. While it's been over a hundred years since Ida B. Wells and Dwight L. Moody overlapped in Chicago, the dynamic they illustrate continues today. In the current cultural moment, black Christians are fighting for more equitable criminal justice policies, immigrant churches are advocating for policies that don't separate asylum-seeking parents from their children, and Native American believers are lamenting as ancient tribal lands are being polluted by oil pipelines. At the same time, there are prominent white Christians publicly debating whether justice, from a biblical vantage point, can ever be social. Some of these leaders wonder whether justice can even be considered Christian when not limited to an individual. As disheartening as this divide is between white Christianity and many Christians of color, white Christianity's tools help us to see why we haven't been able to move past it.

■ ■ ■

Approaching racial segregation and injustice from the perspective of discipleship can move white Christians to a place we have rarely gone—to lived and sacrificial solidarity with our neighbors. There is nothing quick or simple about this. Our definition of discipleship implies the lifelong formation of communities of Christians: *Following Jesus (into the kingdom of God) to become like Jesus (through habit-shaping practices that orient our desires) in order to do what Jesus does.* But for this discipleship to effectively confront the other discipleship of our racialized society, we need to be precise about the challenges that await us. Otherwise, the cultural tools to which white Christianity defaults will undermine our best efforts. So, before moving on, let's see how the reimagined discipleship practices of Part Two that reckon seriously with our racialized society can also overcome the challenges inherent in white Christianity.

Because individualism is the first challenge, it's important to realize that a discipleship approach to racial justice and reconciliation depends on a *community* of Christians. There's nothing especially innovative about this; for generations, Christians have gathered for corporate worship and, by participating in shared liturgical practices such as singing and Holy Communion, have together had their desires aimed toward the kingdom of God. By its very nature the Christian life is communal; individuals find new life within the locally expressed body of Christ. It's not that we lose our individuality when we become Christians, but that who we are as individuals finds fuller and truer expression within the community of saints.

As basic as the corporate nature of the faith is to Christianity, it can be a hard thing to remember in a society that holds individuality as one of its highest values. A number of years ago, as we were just starting our church, one of my mentors told me that the hardest part of planting a church would be simply learning to be the church. This made no sense to me at first—the hardest part of starting a church was just getting a few people to show up! But over time, his wisdom became clear. It's one thing to gather a collection of individuals; it's something else entirely for those individuals to see themselves as a community, as a people with a shared identity who, despite countless differences and disagreements, commit to remaining with one another.

So the discipleship practices that orient us toward the reconciled kingdom of God are *corporate* practices, which means that white Christians must begin thinking of ourselves not only as individuals but also as a group. And in my experience, this is tough! When I talk to white Christians about racial reconciliation or the importance of multicultural ministry, the response is typically enthusiastic. But if I begin talking about white people, white Christianity, or even racial whiteness, the response is tepid or sometimes combative. When mixed with our racialized society, the problem of individualism is that many white people refuse to see ourselves as white. We want to be thought of only as individuals.

In his book *White Awake*, pastor Daniel Hill writes that everyone has a cultural identity. This means that everyone has a way of answering two questions: "'Who am I?' and 'How do I fit into the world?' through the lenses of culture, race, ethnicity, and/or class."[15] As the cultural majority in this country, the problem for white people is that we don't think of ourselves as a distinctive culture but as the neutral standard by which other cultures are categorized. As a white man, I can go through my life unaware of what it means to be white. My assumptions, histories, aspirations, and even my physical representation are portrayed in textbooks and media as the cultural norm.

The ubiquity of white culture makes it a challenging dynamic for white people to claim. Then there is the disturbing way that white culture, when it *is* publicly claimed, is done so by avowed racists and ethnonationalists—hardly the sorts of movements most of us want to be associated with! Despite these real obstacles, for white Christianity to move beyond its segregation, we must recognize our whiteness. We'll look more closely at racial whiteness as we continue. But for now we must acknowledge that we have been born into a world that sees us as racially white and assigns us certain unearned privileges because of it. When I begin a conversation with something like, "As a white man . . ." I am acknowledging the way our racialized society has categorized me and, more difficult to admit, the ways I've internalized this racial sorting. This doesn't mean that I should *only* be known by my white identity; my extended family, diverse neighborhood, and church community are all groups wherein I am shaped and known. But it does mean that, in order to resist the hyperindividualism that typically subverts white Christians' attempts at racial justice, I must come to see that I am not culturally neutral but a member of a particular racial and cultural group.

Because of my commitment to racial justice, I sometimes receive emails from friends and family members with links to heartwarming stories about racial reconciliation. Sometimes these are videos about former avowed racists having been befriended by a person of color and changing their racist ideology. Others have been news stories about white police officers who go out of their way to care for a black or brown young person who needed a helping hand. These emails always make me smile; in the midst of so much racial injustice, any little reason for encouragement goes a long way. But they also point to another of white Christianity's overused tools: relationalism. Because white Christians reduce systemic racial inequity to broken relationships influenced by personal prejudice, the most common approach to addressing racial injustice has to do with building or restoring personal relationships.

Relationships across cultural divides are essential to the biblical vision of reconciliation, but the way personal, individual relationships are elevated in white Christianity above systemic change and social justice is a huge barrier to that same biblical vision. We are right to grieve the segregation within the body of Christ, but as Jennifer Harvey notes,

> The problem of racism—the actual racial situation in our faith communities—is not separateness itself. And togetherness is certainly no solution. Separateness is merely a symptom. The real problem is what our differences represent, how they came to be historically, and what they mean materially and structurally still. Racial separateness is evidence of the extent to which our differences embody legacies of unjust material structures. Racial separateness is a to-be-expected outcome of the reality that our differences literally contain still painful and violent histories that remain unrepressed and unrepaired. Racial separateness reveals that our differences are the very manifestation of ongoing forms of racial injustice and white supremacy. A paradigm that cannot meaningfully incorporate this understanding within its very framing of the problem cannot begin to realize its own hoped-for ends.[16]

The basic problem of relationalism that Harvey notes—that it does not fundamentally address the causes of segregation and injustice—is why we must begin not by pursuing racial diversity but with discipleship. It is also why, as important as racial reconciliation is, our goal is not to make every white church racially diverse but to move these churches toward lived solidarity with the entire body of Christ. By acknowledging and confronting racial discipleship, our reimagined discipleship practices will begin forming communities to confess and confront the conditions that cause segregation and injustice.

This is why focusing on discipleship is not an easy way out for white Christians. Quite the opposite! While welcoming people of color into our congregations or ministries would scratch our relational itch, the underlying factors related to our segregation remain unaddressed. In

contrast, by reorienting our desires and imaginations toward the reconciled kingdom of God—a formation involving the reshaping of long-
held, often unconscious racial habits—we are doing the difficult work
of facing our complicity with the injustices suffered by our family in
Christ. We are also committing to the sacrificial journey of solidarity
that, while certainly relational in character, will lead us to confront the
material sources of our segregation. This is a risky journey, one that
requires deeply formed love for our King and his kingdom.

In addition to individualism and relationalism, the final barrier for us
to account for is antistructuralism. White Christians tend to be skeptical
about the structural nature of racial injustice—preferring to understand
racism through a relational paradigm—as well as structural responses to
injustice and segregation. Yet, as we have seen, racial injustice goes far
beyond strained and broken relationships; it is a reality instilled by the
racial habits that in turn have been oriented by cultural practices infected
with the narrative of racial difference. These practices are sustained in
structures such as governments, schools, and churches.

We cannot afford to ignore the powerful effects of systems and structures in our pursuit of racial reconciliation and justice. In fact, addressing
racial injustice through discipleship practices requires that we elevate the
importance of structures, and not simply for the ways they have warped
our imaginations and desires. To spiritually form white Christians in the
face of racialized cultural structures, our discipleship practices will need
to be sustained by healthy structures of our own. After all, we are not
expecting individual white Christians to disciple themselves out of segregation. Instead, community structures that will continually call white
Christians to faithful discipleship must be built and nurtured.

There are many ways a community could begin to build healthy
structures that take seriously the systemic nature of the racial segregation and injustice we are addressing. For example, a denominational
leader I know has made it a requirement that all of her staff and board
members participate in the denomination's weekend journey through
monuments of the civil rights movement. This intentional experience
exposes these leaders to forgotten parts of our nation's history as well
as to difficult conversations about racial injustice. As a result of these

experiences, this region of the denomination is being led by clergy and lay leaders who share a common experience and language about racial reconciliation. A particular structure has been built that is equipping leaders in their work for a more reconciled and just church.

As we move forward, it's important to remember the discouraging reasons that white Christianity has rarely moved beyond our own segregation to address racial injustice in a meaningful way, even when we've tried. If we are to chart a genuinely new course—one of measurable change in the lives of white Christians and lived solidarity with Christians of color—we must intentionally address these internal barriers. By beginning with discipleship, we are acknowledging white Christianity's dependence on individualism and beginning to see ourselves as a people with a shared culture; we are acknowledging our dependence on relationalism and beginning to confess the systemic roots of our segregation; and we are acknowledging our historic distrust of structures and beginning to build healthy systems and rhythms that sustain our discipleship to Jesus and his reconciled kingdom.

■ ■ ■

Occasionally, when I find myself in the neighborhood, I will pull up beside Ida B. Wells's home, turn off the car, and think about the faithful witness of this courageous woman. Her house has become a local pilgrimage site for me, a place I can go when I need some clarity. In the pursuit of racial reconciliation and justice, I sometimes find myself on the receiving end of some . . . pushback. It turns out that acknowledging the existence of white culture and its unearned privileges, the systemic nature of racial injustice, and the need for white Christians to think structurally about our response to segregation are all good ways to elicit strong responses from some of my fellow white Christians.

Given the cultural tools of white Christianity, I understand where these responses come from, but I still wonder sometimes if I've missed something important. Perhaps I've gone too far. There's no doubt that my work has sometimes been misguided and my motives less than pure. I'm tempted in these moments to retreat to indifference, to allow the concealing nature of my racial whiteness to wash over me.

But then I remember people like Ida B. Wells and Frederick Douglass. Or I think of my many African American colleagues in our neighborhood, pastors and ministry leaders whose biblical theology and lived realities mean they think naturally about systems of racial injustice and structures of healthy resistance to them. I think about the generations of Christians in this country who have wondered how it is that white Christianity remains content in its segregation, paying only occasional lip service to racial justice and reconciliation.

Usually, after a few minutes in front of the old Wells home, I'm ready to get back to work. The noisy voices of pushback have been dialed down and I hear more clearly the voices of generations of Christians like Wells, Douglass, and so many others, urging us toward the just and reconciled kingdom of God.

CHAPTER THREE

WOUNDED BY RACE

ON THE EVENING OF Wednesday, June 17, 2015, the members of
Emanuel African Methodist Episcopal Church in Charleston, South
Carolina, gathered for their weekly prayer meeting. Like churches all
around the country, these women and men joined their pastor for a
short Bible study before praying together. The only thing that made this
Wednesday different for this historic black church was the presence of
a particular young white man. He'd walked in as the study began, asking
for the pastor. That pastor, Rev. Clementa C. Pinckney, invited the
visitor to sit next to him for the next hour of the Bible study.

"Black churches," writes Austin Channing Brown, "are gracious and
hospitable, loving and welcoming, filled with people who like hugs and
can't wait for the opportunity to speak goodness into your life."[1] That
Wednesday night, the white visitor was a recipient of that gracious and
hospitable welcome. He was warmly received, notes Anthony Szczesiul,
despite the history he represented. "Given the long history of this black
church in the south, given the fraught history of racial discrimination and
violence in the nation, and given the church members' probable own life
experiences (some were elderly and had lived under Jim Crow segregation), self-interest may have dictated caution when facing an unknown
white man, but . . . they unconditionally welcomed this stranger in."[2]

I have experienced the hospitality of black churches countless times,
and I never cease to be moved by the graciousness of their welcome.

Our congregation's location in an African American neighborhood means I'm often one of the few white people in a community meeting or a clergy get-together. I've been invited to preach to black congregations and have been mentored by black pastors who continually affirm my gifts and push back my insecurities.

And it's not just black churches that have extended undeserved hospitality my way. A few years ago I was a guest preacher at a new Spanish-speaking church, stumbling through the sermon in my very out-of-practice Spanish. The congregation listened attentively, helpfully calling out words when I got lost. I've rarely felt so loved and encouraged. A year or so later, I visited another Latino/a church during a time when immigrants were being publicly disparaged and scapegoated. I knew from conversations with their pastors that many of his church members were afraid; some would no longer come to the evening church services, too anxious to leave their homes in the predominantly white community after dark. Yet despite their understandable anxieties and the xenophobia they had experienced, the congregation embraced me. After the service they brought me down to the church basement where we feasted over a potluck dinner. There, in that small-town church basement, surrounded by families who had risked hazardous journeys to come to this country, I experienced and understood the biblical "right hand of fellowship" that Paul mentions in Galatians 2:9.

It wasn't until the members of Emanuel AME closed their eyes in prayer that the visitor took out his gun and, racial epithets streaming from his mouth, murdered Rev. Pinckney and eight other church members: Tywanza Sanders, Cynthia Hurd, Rev. Sharonda Coleman-Singleton, Myra Thompson, Ethel Lance, Rev. Daniel Simmons, Rev. DePayne Middleton-Doctor, and Susie Jackson. The visitor repaid their kindness with death and then fled into the night.

I think about the hospitality that was violated so traumatically in Charleston when I read about the experiences of people of color who attend white churches. In the previous chapter we saw how difficult this experience can be, especially during times of public racial injustice. Such was the case during the 2016 presidential campaign. As it became evident that Donald Trump—a man with a public history of racial bias and anti-immigrant sentiment—would be a major-party nominee, many of these Christians wondered how their voices and experiences could be so easily ignored by the white Christians with whom they worshiped every week. Watching the campaign unfold from our own multiracial church, a black woman who is one of our leaders turned to me on the way out of church one Sunday. With sadness in her voice, she asked, "How can so many white Christians support this man?" I mumbled something in response, but I'd been wondering the same thing, and I didn't have much to say. If my experiences in black churches and immigrant ministries had been marked by great hospitality, it seemed we were seeing the opposite play out in white Christianity— exclusion, protection, and defensiveness. The worship leader and I walked toward our cars silently; I don't think she expected an answer.

■ ■ ■

White Christianity has generally failed to make disciples of God's reconciled kingdom: people who follow Jesus to become like Jesus in order to do what Jesus does. Our collective failure to acknowledge and account for the racial practices that shape our desires and imaginations has led to segregation within the body of Christ. Rather than resisting the sinful narrative of racial difference, we have left people to be oriented away from the reconciled kingdom of God by habits that are constantly being shaped—and warped—by our racialized society. Our dependence on the tools of individualism, relationalism, and antistructuralism mean that when white Christianity *has* tried to tackle segregation and racial justice, our efforts have typically failed or simply perpetuated white cultural assumptions.

About the connection between inadequate discipleship and injustice Dallas Willard wrote,

> The lack of concern for social justice, where that is evident, itself requires an explanation. And the current position of the church in our world may by better explained by what liberals and conservatives have shared, than by how they differ. For different reasons, and with different emphases, they have agreed that

discipleship to Christ is optional to membership in the Christian church. Thus the very type of life that could change the course of human society—and upon occasion has done so—is excluded from the essential message of the church.[3]

Once we see white Christianity's complicity with racial segregation and injustice, it is our urgent responsibility to reimagine our discipleship practices such that our communities are oriented toward the reconciled kingdom of God.

However, before turning to these practices, we must reflect on how the segregation and racial injustice inherent to white Christianity have wreaked real-world havoc. It's been my experience that an especially strong trait of white Christianity is our impulse to move forward quickly, or to try to fix what we perceive to be broken. We then wonder, often with frustration or defensiveness, why others are still stuck in the past. After all, slavery was a long time ago, right? We prefer not to linger. Yet the discipleship journey to redirect our desires toward the reconciled kingdom of God cannot be rushed. Our emotions must be fully engaged. After all, our discipleship paradigm is deeply concerned with our affections and loves. As desiring beings, it is our hearts that need transformation, and this cannot be accomplished simply by receiving new information. We need to *feel* the impact of our segregation on our own lives as well as on the lives of people of color and their communities. In other words, we need to lament.

Understanding the big-ness of racial discipleship is essential to understanding the extent of the problem, as well as the importance of reimagining Christian discipleship practices that direct us toward solidarity. There is a danger in this approach, though. By focusing so persistently on the systemic nature of race and racism, we can miss the embodied nature of the problem we face. We must not allow our focus on the big picture to distract us from the actual decisions white Christians make, which produce particular hardships and sufferings in other people's lives. Yes, it is true that we have been racially discipled by a deceived and destructive society. But it's also true that this discipleship is expressed and encouraged by the decisions we ourselves make. And these choices, hard as this may be to confess, reveal our complicity with the racialized society that has long been at work on our desires and imaginations.

Author Ta-Nehisi Coates, in an especially vivid passage in his book *Between the World and Me*, writes that it can be easy to make racism an abstraction. "But," he writes, "all our phrasing—race relations, racial chasm, racial justice, racial profiling, white privilege, even white supremacy—serves to obscure that racism is a visceral experience, that it dislodges brains, blocks airways, rips muscle, extracts organs, cracks bones, breaks teeth. You must never look away from this."[4] Coates is addressing his black teenage son, but we white Christians must heed his difficult counsel as well. We must not look away.

■ ■ ■

Those who have suffered the worst of racism deserve our sustained attention. Horrifying experiences of land theft, enforced cultural assimilation, kidnapping into slavery, lynching, legally enforced segregation, police brutality, and countless other examples from our racialized society deserve our sustained attention. But because our aim is to disciple white Christians away from our racial segregation, we will first consider some of the ways white people have been deceived and damaged by the narrative of racial difference.

We tend to think of racism as proceeding from racial difference but, as we will see, it is racial animus fueled by the desire for power and superiority that led to what we understand as race today. It was sinful attempts to dehumanize fellow image-bearers of God for economic gain that led Europeans to develop complicated and constantly shifting theories of racial difference. And while the theories evolved, the one constant was that white people were always found at the top of the racial hierarchy, and black people were put at the bottom. Racism is prejudice based on socially constructed differences in order to benefit some while oppressing others. Anyone can be prejudiced, but in the American story, only those with access to the controlling power of whiteness can be racist.

But who, exactly, was white? This too was a complicated question, with different nationalities, cultures, and ethnicities finding themselves outside the boundaries of whiteness only to eventually make their way in. Two things were required for entry. The first was to abandon long-held identity markers for the blunt category of racial whiteness. The price of the ticket for admission to the American community, writes Baldwin, "was to become 'white.' No one was white before he/she came to America. It took generations, and a vast amount of coercion, before this became a white country."[5] For example, somewhere in my own ethnic background is a mix of German, Swedish, and English along with some Russian cultural heritage and a family line that traces through the Confederacy. Yet very little if any of this consciously affects how I live day to day. In other words, I'm white.[6]

It's hard for us to understand how groundbreaking this development was. When European immigrants shed culture and ethnicity in order to gain promises of whiteness, they were going against something deep within their humanity. The particularities of culture, ethnicity, and language are all gifts from God, results of humanity's formation by the creation itself. These God-ordained differences are the good results of God's command to spread throughout the earth as stewards of creation. Yet now, in order to access the promises of the American Dream, immigrants were required to replace the diversities of these God-glorifying particularities with a one-size-fits-all category: whiteness.

Of course, there was no manual given to new immigrants to America about climbing the racial hierarchy. It's not as though someone explained to each new citizen how they would need to set aside the particularities of culture and ethnicity in order to achieve the American Dream. These assumptions were simply a part of the air that everyone breathed, the rules of the game internalized by anyone hoping to get ahead in this new land. Rather than understanding themselves through their own long and complex histories, usually involving specific places, these new Americans would come to see themselves simply as white, a bargain that also required their disdain for those labeled black.

This is the other price demanded by racial whiteness: complicity in its destructive rationale. Becoming white, Coates tells his son, "was not achieved through wine tasting and ice-cream socials, but rather through the flaying of backs; the chaining of limbs; the strangling of dissidents; the destruction of families; the rape of mothers; the sale of children; and various other acts meant, first and foremost, to deny you and me the right to secure and govern our own bodies."[7] Achieving whiteness and access to the top of the racial hierarchy meant aligning oneself against the very humanity of Native Americans, enslaved Africans, and those immigrants who, at any given point in time, were deemed unworthy of whiteness. "Throughout our immigration history," writes Ken Wytsma, "you can trace a pattern of how races or ethnicities were demonized and excluded. When we fear a certain group, we exclude them—and then, once we feel okay with that ethnic group, we demonize another."[8]

This history can be almost too painful for many white people to acknowledge. In her collection of essays about race, Eula Biss writes about how elusive the meaning of whiteness is to those of us who are white. "[It] isn't easy to accept the legacy of whiteness as an identity. It is an identity that carries the burden of history without fostering a true understanding of the painfulness and the cost of complicity. That's why so many of us try to pretend that to be white is merely to be raceless."[9]

I know what she means. Each year I cofacilitate a cross-racial journey to important places from the civil rights movement. The trip is a kind of pilgrimage with the goal of leading participants further down the road of racial reconciliation. At the beginning of the trip, we ask each of the thirty or so participants to answer this question: How do you identify racially or ethnically?

As we go around the circle, most of the African Americans have no problem answering quickly and succinctly. The same is true for most of the other people of color. The white people, on the other hand, often struggle with this question. People identify themselves as Euro-American, Anglo-American, or Caucasian. Some go into long histories about where the different branches of their family tree immigrated from. Some try to get away with, "I'm a child of God." No one, it seems, *wants* to identify themselves as white. Those that do often say the word quickly, as though they can't expel it quickly enough from their mouths.

It's true that whiteness carries the burden of history while also working to distract us from the ugliness of that history, including its legacy to this day. So we look away. We allow ourselves to forget. We don't question the existence of the racial hierarchy that is evidenced in almost every metric related to the qualities of our lives. We allow our nation's racial practices to warp our imaginations and then to conceal the very ways we've been deformed.

Of all the ways we have been damaged by whiteness, I believe the most significant is the chasm we have opened between ourselves and people of color, other image-bearers of the living God. Rather than listening to our neighbors' stories of the harm inflicted on their communities by race, we often explain away their experiences. We appeal to our own racial enlightenment as proof that we are not racists and thus bear no responsibility for the harm done to our neighbors by a racialized society. Worse, sometimes we don't even believe our neighbors and friends of color when they explain what it's like to live beyond the boundaries of whiteness. "There is a long history," writes Drew G. I. Hart, "going all the way back to slavery, of white Americans not trusting black perspectives as truthful."[10] The regularity with which white conversation partners dismiss what I share about the experiences of my friends of color is one indication of the distrust sown by whiteness.

It's a tricky thing to say that white people have been damaged by racism. Obviously, there is no equivalency between this idea and the suffering inflicted by white people and our racialized society upon the lives and communities of people of color. And yet, the very process of becoming white—leaving behind cultural particularity for the malevolent promises of the racial hierarchy—cannot but wound those of us who've come to imagine ourselves as white. In his short book detailing his own exploration of whiteness, the agrarian author Wendell Berry points out that, "If the white man has inflicted the wound of racism upon black men, the cost has been that he would receive the mirror image of that wound into himself. As the master, or as a member of the dominant race, he has felt little compulsion to acknowledge it or speak of it; the more painful it has grown the more deeply he has hidden it within himself."[11]

We are a damaged people. In the past, most of us have ignored the hidden wound, the result of our devilish bargain for controlling power. We don't think of ourselves as privileged, as having been given a leg up at someone else's expense. But if we will be still long enough, we might begin to sense the damage we carry, the damage with which we are complicit, the damage we've inflicted. And if we choose to trust the voices and experiences of people of color, our capacity to feel this damage will grow, and with it, our ability to challenge the destructive demands of whiteness.

■ ■ ■

In my experiences with racial reconciliation conversations, there usually comes a moment when superficial talk gets real. Often this comes about because a person of color takes the risk to share how racism and white supremacy have impacted her life. And then, almost invariably, in response to this vulnerable testimony, a white person begins to speak, usually through tears. This person shares about how overwhelming this experience has been, how he hadn't known the extent of our racialized society and its racist history, about how sad, angry, or confused he is feeling now. I've watched this happen so many times that I can almost predict it: the move away from a person of color's experience to a white person's emotions.

I have experienced these strong emotions myself, but as Austin Channing Brown points out, focusing on white emotions rather than the experiences of people of color can be dangerous. She writes, "If Black people are dying in the street, we must consult with white feelings before naming the evils of police brutality. If white family members are being racist, we must take Grandpa's feelings into account before we proclaim our objections to such speech. . . . White fragility protects whiteness and forces Black people to fend for themselves."[12] So I don't want this book—a book focused on white Christians—to become another exercise in which the emotions of white people take priority over the experiences of people of color.

But it's a delicate balance. We must lament the legacy of racial whiteness without succumbing to its emotionally consuming gravity. It's not shame we are pursuing here, but responsibility.

And for what are we responsible? What provokes our lament? We have seen some of the ways that the narrative of racial difference, institutionalized by our society's powerful structures, have created and enforced a racial hierarchy that impacts the quality of life of individuals and communities. This is not to say that white people in America do not face injustices, even systemic ones—only that we don't face them *because of our race*. As white Christians, beneficiaries of this racial hierarchy, we are responsible to see things that our race works overtime to make us miss. We are responsible to see the inequities of our public school systems, the disparities in our criminal justice system, the yawning gap between the generational wealth of white people and people of color, the ongoing impact of redlining and housing segregation, the legacy of discrimination that runs through many of our law enforcement departments, and the inequalities in the realm of health. And, most importantly, we are responsible to see and understand that none of these injustices can be rightly interpreted without accounting for the presence of race.

White Christians must learn to see the visceral and embodied nature of these sins. Racism, writes Hart, is a psychological burden in which a person of color's psyche is "routinely attacked and crushed in our society."[13] The end result of racism is to wreak havoc on the lives of particular people. It is an attack on the bodies and minds of women and men created in the image of God. It is dehumanizing. It is demonic. Therefore we must not look away.

Because our racialized society is also sexist, the burden of racism falls most heavily on women. This too is a reality we must not turn from. I'm thinking of the African American woman who is the only black person and the only woman in her workplace, negotiating the remarks and stereotypes that remain invisible to her coworkers. Or the Mexican-American woman who works in an office of the federal government, and the dismay she felt watching the portrait of our new president being hung in her office's lobby. Each day she walks past the image of a man who slandered her people, calling them criminals, drug dealers, and rapists.[14] Or the mothers who I've marched with through the streets of our city, protesting the gun violence that plagues our economically disenfranchised and structurally isolated communities. Some carry framed pictures of their slain sons, young black men whose murderers will likely never be prosecuted. They live without closure, feeling the constant reminder of how little their children mattered to those with the power to protect them. I think also about the ninth-grade girl who told us her summer plans revolved around caring for a friend who had recently been seriously wounded, another victim of the gun violence that fires into those confined to our hypersegregated neighborhoods.

In the face of persistent racism, many of these women hold together families and neighborhoods; they encourage their children's education in less-than-ideal schools while pursuing their own; they are the hands and feet of countless churches. They are, as theologian Chanequa Walker-Barnes describes them, strong. But she notes this is a strength required by survival in a hostile society. "It is a racialized gender performance, a scripted role . . . usually beginning in childhood."[15] And this armor of strength, though necessary, obscures the damage of racism on the female body: "Black women are experiencing epidemic rates of medical conditions such as obesity, diabetes, hypertension, and HIV/AIDS. And they have higher morbidity and mortality rates than any other racial-gender group for nearly every major cause of death."[16] Though blatant racist symbols like the Ku Klux Klan and lynching trees have faded from our memories, racism continues to maim and kill, and those who suffer the most are often black women and other women of color.

While there are good reasons we often speak about the impact of race and racism on African Americans, given the insidious and pervasive narrative of racial difference, we should expect there to be detrimental impacts of *anyone* who cannot or will not claim the protection of whiteness. Yet those who are neither black nor white—Asian Americans and Latinos/as for example—often find themselves on the outside looking in when it comes to finding a place within the nation's complicated racial landscape. Author Jeff Change writes that, "On matters of race, America teaches everyone to think in binaries—zero or one, this or that. There is no in-between."[17] Yet from its American inception, racial whiteness impacted everyone. About Native Americans Hart writes, "The presence of the original hosts of the land constituted a threat to white identity and the sense of America as a 'white country.'"[18] No matter whether your presence in this land preceded the European colonialists, your ancestors came here willingly, or your lineage is traced through people who were kidnapped into slavery, racial whiteness has thoroughly altered your life.

The damage inflicted by race and racism on the communities of particular people is incalculable. And this is where the damage done to white people and the wounds suffered by people of color begin to overlap. Once white people begin to understand the scope of racial injustice, writes Wendell Berry, "once you begin to awaken to the realities of what you know, you are subject to staggering recognitions of your own complicity in history and in the events of your own life."[19] And though the awakening is painful to those of us accustomed to slumbering through this racialized society, though we will be strongly tempted to return to our illusions of meritocracies and colorblindness, if we choose to make peace with the pain and resist the slumber, we will find ourselves waking up to the reconciled kingdom of God.

■ ■ ■

As we pursue a discipleship to Jesus that leads us from segregation to solidarity with those we have wounded, white Christians must become accustomed to the very thing whiteness has insulated us from: uncomfortable truth. There is nothing easy about this. "Collusion is written onto our way of life," Eula Biss writes, "and nearly every interaction among white people is an invitation to collusion."[20] This is our lament, that for too long we have not resisted racial injustice, being unwilling to sacrifice the privileges of our race for genuine community with our sisters and brothers in Christ. This too is our responsibility, to confess our complicity with injustice and move forward even as our hearts continue to lament.

The focus of our lament sharpens when we are willing to honestly consider our collusion. After all, there's no reason more white Christians couldn't have stood against racism and white supremacy at any point in the past. There's no reason churches and ministries couldn't have identified the deceptive narrative of racial difference and publicly and intentionally opposed it. There's no reason we couldn't have discovered the ways this nation's racial practices were deforming us away from the reconciled kingdom of God and leaving us content in our segregation. Yet rather than resisting this deforming discipleship, the vast majority of white Christianity has gone along with it. We have colluded with injustice. We are complicit in the suffering experienced by our sisters and brothers in Christ.

"White people can be exhausting," writes Channing Brown.[21] And though she surely means all white people, she especially has Christians in mind. For people of color, white Christianity has rarely offered the emotionally safe and dignity-affirming space that should be expected in our communities. Our unwillingness to challenge society's racial discipleship along with our dependence on a limiting set of cultural tools with which to pursue reconciliation has severely limited white Christianity's hospitality. Additionally, our very history—which is generally unacknowledged and, thus, unchallenged—is one of racial exclusion. The black church only exists because of the racist exclusion of white Christianity. The Reverend Richard Allen, for example, established the African Methodist Episcopal Church in 1816 not because the black citizens of Philadelphia wanted a racially homogenous church but because their full participation was unwelcome and opposed in the white churches.

Though most white Christians saw nothing wrong with the segregation born in their churches, for black Christians such as Ida B. Wells and Frederick Douglass the hypocrisy and damage could not be missed. In the appendix to his *Life of an American Slave*, Douglass called the faith of America's white citizens "slaveholding religion" and, he wrote, "between the Christianity of this land, and the Christianity of Christ, I recognize the widest possible difference—so wide, that to receive the one as good, pure, and holy, is of necessity to reject the other as bad, corrupt, and wicked." How was it possible, wondered the abolitionist, to have,

> men-stealers for ministers, women-whippers for missionaries, and cradle-plunderers for church members. The man who wields the blood-clotted cowskin during the week fills the pulpit on Sunday, and claims to be a minister of the meek and lowly Jesus. The man who robs me of my earnings at the end of each week meets me as a class-leader on Sunday morning, to show me the

way of life, and the path of salvation. He who sells my sister, for purposes of prostitution, stands forth as the pious advocate of purity. He who proclaims it a religious duty to read the Bible denies me the right of learning to read the name of the God who made me. He who is the religious advocate of marriage robs whole millions of its sacred influence, and leaves them to the ravages of wholesale pollution. [22]

If the sacrificial welcome shown by the members of Emanuel AME in Charleston has its precedent in the black churches that risked everything to provide hospitality to those who had been racially oppressed and excluded, should we not wonder about the historical roots of present-day expressions of white Christianity? Though most of our churches and ministries do not intentionally support the sorts of injustices identified by Douglass, do we actually believe that we bear none of the exclusionary traits of our racial ancestors?

White churches that attempt to welcome people of color often perpetuate the cultural assumptions and biases of racial whiteness. And while the big-picture dynamics that we've investigated are at work in these situations—things like the white Christian toolkit and an unwillingness to challenge racial discipleship—white Christianity's racially exclusive nature also includes the decisions made by the individuals who make it up. Sociologists have shown how white Christians "initiate utility-based race tests to determine whether people of color are willing to serve the interests of whites in the space, or execute exclusionary race tests to coerce people of color into leaving the space."[23] Christians of color are examined when entering white Christian spaces, and these tests serve either to ensure that a person of color will conform to white norms or to make it clear that she is not welcome at all.

Of course, the racially exclusionary history of white Christianity is no longer tenable in a society that publicly decries racism and embraces multiculturalism. In a society that sees itself as colorblind, white Christians walk a tricky tightrope of maintaining our culturally white spaces while including enough people of color to protect us from being seen as racists. This is where the race tests come in—subtle conversations or cultural dynamics that force people of color to conform or leave.

Colleta Rhoads, a cross-cultural missionary who identifies as mixed-race, describes an encounter in her mostly white church that illustrates how race tests work.

We took our seats after worship and welcomed our pastor on stage. His messages, always peppered with humor, drew me in. I can't recall the particulars that morning, but I found myself in an auditorium of a thousand people, dumbfounded at the words coming from the pulpit. Pastor was making fun of Native Americans, throwing out cheap stereotypes. And for what? I leaned forward and glanced at the rest of my family; looks of shock and disbelief were worn on all their faces. I leaned back slowly and waited for the event to pass. I heard nothing else of the sermon that day; I just sat in the house of God and cried. It was clear that day that I was not even safe at church; even here the ugly root of prejudice had infiltrated.[24]

Despite her genuine desire to participate in the life of this church, Rhoads understood clearly the cost her family would be required to pay. Her painful experience illustrates the important interplay between the structures of racism and the personal choices that sustain them. It's not enough to understand the racial discipleship that has led to our segregation; white Christians must also be honest about our own specific complicities with racial injustice.

We have contributed to the segregation of the body of Christ. Rather than standing as a source of reconciliation and justice, we have aided and abetted white Christianity's participation in the divisive and destructive aims of our racialized society. Our racially discipled imaginations have led us away from solidarity, fostering an unthinking complicity with the suffering experienced by other members of the body of Christ. Wendell Berry laments, "Far from curing the wound of racism, the white man's Christianity has been its soothing bandage—a bandage masquerading as Sunday clothes, for the wearing of which one expects a certain moral credit."[25]

■ ■ ■

We are pursuing something far better than moral credit here. It is a truer experience of the kingdom of God that compels us to confess these painful realities. As we turn to the reimagined discipleship practices that hold the potential of leading our imaginations and desires away from segregation to solidarity, we do so with grief in our hearts. We confess our collusion with injustice and complicity with segregation. We remember that the systems and structures that have discipled our racial imaginations have damaged the lives and communities of our sisters and brothers in Christ. We remember, too, that these systems and structures require our choices and actions.

There is hope, but it's a kind of hope that whiteness has obscured from us. Within the glare of endless injustices we must not look away; we must not pretend that the distraction of superficial optimism is the same thing as biblical hope. "Instead of waiting for the bright sunshine," writes Channing Brown, "I have learned to rest in the shadow of hope."[26] It is in this shadow of hope, rescued from the delusions and illusions of whiteness, that we will find our place within the community of saints. There is suffering within this shadow but solidarity as well. We should expect nothing less from the body of Christ.

... TO TRUE SOLIDARITY.

BECAUSE IT HAS BEEN DEFECTIVE DISCIPLESHIP that has led to white Christianity's segregation, we must begin not by pursuing racial, ethnic, or cultural diversity but by addressing our discipleship practices. As James K. A. Smith puts it, "Christian worship needs to be intentionally liturgical, formative, and pedagogical in order to *counter* such mis-formations and misdirections.... Christian worship functions as a counter-formation to the mis-formation of secular liturgies into which we are 'thrown' from an early age."[1] This is our task in Part Two, to reimagine discipleship practices that will lead white Christians away from segregation by shaping the habits which orient our imaginations toward the kingdom of God.

We are focused on practices because of how human beings actually move through the world, compelled by our desires. The emphasis is on flesh-and-blood people participating together in the practices of Christian worship so that we are directed away from segregation. This is not a kind of social determinism in which people change simply as a result of doing the same thing over and over again. Rather, as with generations of Christians before us, we come to these practices anticipating the Holy Spirit to breathe new life into our lungs, new visions into our imaginations.

We are also elevating practices because they hold the possibility of resisting white Christianity's inadequate tools—individualism, relationalism, and antistructuralism—which have previously failed to meaningfully address our segregation. By their very nature, reimagining our practices will require us to embrace our place within a community. We cannot *only* think individually or relationally, and we must acknowledge the power of structures to either deform or re-form our imaginations in relation to the kingdom of God. As such, the discipleship practices we'll explore in the coming chapters can help us restrain the instincts within white Christianity that have sabotaged previous attempts at racial reconciliation.

■ ■ ■

The goal of our reimagined discipleship practices is *solidarity* with the body of Christ. The move to solidarity is a reflection of Paul's command in Romans 12:15: "Rejoice with those who rejoice; mourn with those who mourn." We hear it in his joyful commendation of the Macedonian churches, who, "in the midst of a very severe trial, their overflowing joy and their extreme poverty welled up in rich generosity" as they gave to meet the needs of their fellow Christians (2 Corinthians 8:2).

Christian solidarity is empathetic and embodied. It is potentially costly and deeply caring. Despite chasms such as distance, nationality, and language, the early churches prioritized visible solidarity as an expression of their shared place within the body of Christ.

There are two reasons for white Christianity—churches, fellowships, ministries—to pursue solidarity rather than first seeking to become multiracial/ethnic/cultural. First, as we have already seen, racial segregation is less about separateness than about the material damages of our racially unjust society. It is possible to build a multiracial ministry that leaves structures of racism and white supremacy totally undisturbed. In fact, it is easy for multiracial churches to bend toward the comfort of white people rather than the well-being of people of color. Focusing on solidarity moves the focus away from shallow togetherness onto the priorities and flourishing of Christians of color. "White American Christians in our society," writes Drew G. I. Hart, "must do something seemingly absurd and unnatural, yet very Christian in orientation: they must move decisively toward a counterintuitive solidarity with those on the margins. They must allow the eyes of the violated of the land to lead and guide them, seeking to have renewed minds no longer conformed to the patterns of our world."[2]

The second reason for making solidarity our goal is that every expression of white Christianity can pursue gospel reconciliation immediately. Rather than outsourcing this essential Christian vocation to multiracial churches or to congregations in urban or racially diverse regions, every white congregation can contribute to the unity of the body of Christ across lines of cultural division. In fact, given what we have observed about the particular injustices associated with racial whiteness, it's not a stretch to say that white churches have a front-lines role in the spiritual battle for reconciliation.

Our focus on solidarity does not downplay the important possibilities of white churches embarking on the slow and costly journey to becoming multiracial in order to bear witness to the kingdom of God. But by elevating solidarity as our objective, we acknowledge a simple fact that Christians of color have long known: for the American church to experience genuine reconciliation, white Christianity must play its unique and indispensable role of discipling white Christians away from injustice and segregation.

If discipleship practices offer the means to lead us from segregation to solidarity, lament provides the mood. We dare not come to this ministry of reconciliation with any other posture. We move forward humbly, as those only slowly awakening to the extent of the damage done by our previously defective discipleship.

The road ahead will often feel unnatural to those of us who've been discipled in the narrative of racial difference. For those who've known only racial privilege, the journey toward equitable reconciliation will sting at times. We are accustomed to segregation, novices on this journey to solidarity. And so we must practice.

■ ■ ■

To be effective, the discipleship practices to which we now turn require courageous leadership. I was once asked by a group of mostly white leaders representing a large evangelistic organization how they could know if they were making strides toward racial reconciliation. I must have been tired, because my blunt reply was something like, "You'll know you're actually making a difference when some white people leave your organization and others stop supporting you financially."

It's probably not what they were expecting to hear, but despite my lack of tact, I'm sticking with my answer. Any majority white organization, Christian or not, that challenges the long-held and accepted norms of our racialized society is bound to face opposition—sometimes significantly so.

In recent years, as instances of racial injustice have received more public attention, ministry leaders have tried to speak truthfully to their white communities. This has sometimes taken the form of a public confession about racial inequity or a biblical teaching about the priority of reconciliation as evidence of God's righteousness. Most of the time when leaders such as these take a public stand against racial injustice— especially when they explicitly identify the sins associated with racial whiteness—they are met with resistance. Their commitment to the gospel might be questioned. Or they will be urged to stop confusing politics with their faith. They will be encouraged—strongly!—to stick to the so-called essentials of the faith.

Sadly, because these godly leaders had not anticipated this level of opposition, they often pull back. The reasons for their retreat are many and, without walking in their shoes, we should be slow to assume that we'd do any differently faced with similar resistance. What is important for us as we intentionally confront the sources of our segregation is to prepare soberly for the spiritual battle ahead.

Though the practices themselves must always be communal, the exercise of leadership will often be solitary. There is rarely affirmation, at least from within white Christianity, for those leaders who make the connection between our faith and the sins of our race. A leader who is convinced of the righteousness of this work must be prepared for discomfort, loneliness, and opposition. When people and their money leave, it will seem like we made a mistake. The temptation to return to the status quo of our racial divisions will be strong. But for those who count the cost at the beginning of the journey, these hardships will simply become a part of our own discipleship to the crucified Savior. What might have otherwise turned us around will instead become beautiful parts of the testimonies we will one day share about our journey toward solidarity with the body of Christ.

■ ■ ■

When our youngest son was three, he developed an interest in volcanoes. Perhaps *obsession* is a better word. He wanted us to read him books about volcanoes and find pictures online of volcanic mountains around the world. Though he was still learning to talk, his vocabulary began including the names of these far-flung volcanoes, as well as volcanic terminology: magma, lava, and even pyroclastic flow. Neither my older son, my wife, nor I shared this passion, but we all dutifully engaged the budding volcanologist and soon we too had developed storehouses of volcanic knowledge.

About a year later our family drove to Washington state for a three-month family sabbatical. Knowing that we'd be relatively close to Mount St. Helens, my wife planned a two-night camping trip for us near the volcano. Of course, our son was thrilled with this plan, and the rest of us enjoyed his excitement. But something interesting happened as we began to drive up the narrow road toward the mountain. We were all excited. We were pointing out geological features that we'd read about as we peered around the winding curves, hoping for a first glimpse of the crater.

And then, suddenly, there it was. We had come on a beautiful day, and from the distance Mount St. Helens rose to greet us. We were all, very literally, in awe. We spent the rest of the day hiking around the mountain, listening to park rangers describe its dramatic history, and lingering at the overlook as the sun went down, watching this giant volcano glow softly in the dusk.

You see, our three-year-old son had discipled our family into loving volcanoes. The practices of reading about volcanoes, checking out every single book in the Chicago Public Library system about volcanoes, and watching nature videos about volcanoes had shaped our habits. Soon we were talking about volcanoes even when my son wasn't around. We'd bring up a fascinating fact about volcanic geology with unsuspecting friends. And of course, it seemed like the most normal thing in the world to plan a camping trip at the base of an active volcano simply because we were already within a few hundred miles of it.

As we approached Mount St. Helens that August morning, I realized that all that discipleship had oriented my desires and imagination in a new direction. Yes, we had come all that way for the three-year-old, but now *I* wanted to be there too. I looked around the mountainous landscape through a different lens, seeing the awe-inspiring features I'd certainly have missed without my son's discipling presence.

We did a lot of amazing things during that three-month sabbatical, but would you believe me if I told you that Mount St. Helens was my favorite? This is the power of leadership when it comes to these reimagined discipleship practices. Even when no one else sees the need for a change, a leader will move forward courageously, introducing the practices that can shape the habits that will then aim desires and imaginations toward the reconciled kingdom of God.

■ ■ ■

Finally, before we turn to the practices themselves, I want to offer two caveats: one about my choice of these specific practices and the other about how I will describe them. First, I need to admit that the discipleship practices in the coming chapters have been selected somewhat arbitrarily. These practices are not necessarily the essential marks of a church. They do not line up with the sacraments. In other words, there is not anything especially unique about these practices as opposed to other biblically rooted practices that communities of Christians participate in together. Rather, I've selected these particular discipleship practices because they are common to most church and ministry settings and because they offer relatively straightforward connections with our goal of discipling white Christians into solidarity with the body of Christ. There are certainly other practices that can also do this re-forming work; these happen to be most easily accessible to a wide range of contexts. It's my hope that as a community begins down this road, its members will soon find other practices that hold the same latent potential to orient them more deeply toward the reconciled kingdom of God. The principles behind these particular practices are applicable to other corporate practices that churches depend on to disciple their people.

This leads to my second caveat. Each of the subsequent chapters reimagines a discipleship practice. To do this, I will provide suggestions for how each practice can be practically engaged with in order to re-form habits and desires away from segregation and racial injustice. My hope, though, is that readers will think of these suggestions as starting points. In the same way that the practices themselves are not meant to be comprehensive, my suggestions should be thought of as the beginning of a conversation. The particularities of any given context—the history of your town, the ages of those who make up your ministry, the current movement of the Holy Spirit, and so on—should provide creative fodder for how these discipleship practices can be reimagined to most effectively direct a community toward the reconciled kingdom of God.

CHAPTER FOUR

PRACTICING
TABLE FELLOWSHIP

EACH SUMMER OUR CHURCH takes a retreat. For one weekend we leave the hustle of Chicago for a calm Wisconsin lake. This ritual is a time for community building, rest, and play. There's always a lot of laughing and good conversations. It's a chance for our urban, multiracial congregation to take a collective breath, remember the good work and worship to which we've been called, and enjoy our community. But in 2015 we had a very different kind of retreat.

The nine members of Emanuel AME had been gunned down in their church a few short days before we drove away from the city in Friday rush hour traffic. We arrived at the retreat center in states ranging from sadness to despair to rage. Rather than beginning with icebreakers and games as we typically do, we sat in a circle to give people a chance to express what they were experiencing.

It was a heavy evening. The rest of the two-day retreat proceeded mostly as normal, though we continued to think about the specter of a white man desecrating the sacredness of that church with his murderous hatred.

On the Sunday morning of our retreat just before we return home, we typically share testimonies about what we heard from God during the weekend. We end by serving one another Holy Communion. But as people began to share, it quickly became evident that this wouldn't be a typical Sunday morning. Rather than talk about the retreat, our members mostly described how they were processing the church massacre. One black man, a sheriff, told us how hard it was for him to leave behind his gun whenever he went anywhere, even when he was off-duty. But the retreat had become a sacred space for him, and during previous years he had left his weapon home. Not this year, he told us. After what had happened in that Charleston sanctuary, no place felt safe to this husband and father. An Asian-American man shared about his grief and confusion about knowing how to appropriately enter the pain felt by his African-American sisters and brothers. While he has known prejudice and discrimination, the racial violence exhibited in Charleston was beyond his comprehension. How was he to respond? Knowing we would soon be sharing Communion, a black woman wondered if she could come to the table. Her anger was too strong, she said. It didn't seem right for her to receive the bread and cup.

We were running short on time, so Pastor Michelle Dodson and I transitioned to the Communion liturgy. We led our grieving and angry community through the familiar prayers and readings. And then came the moment I will never forget. As I lifted up the broken loaf, Pastor Michelle began to say those familiar words from 1 Corinthians 10:17, recited by churches around the world every Sunday: "Because there is one loaf, we, who are many, are one body, for we all share the one loaf." Except this time she couldn't finish the sentence. The words *are one body* caught in her throat.

She stood there silently, our African-American pastor, her tears a reflection of many other faces in the room. The apparent impossibility, absurdity even, of these words were obvious to each of us. Could we really confess this biblical unity in the shadow of the Charleston massacre? How, within a society where black Christians could not feel physically safe even in church, could we imagine that we were really one body? In a moment when the divisive power of race was so evident, when evil seemed so strong, how were we to proclaim the power of Christ's body and blood to make us one?

A long and quiet moment passed. Then Pastor Michelle finished the liturgy, and one by one, people began to share the Lord's Supper with each other. "This is the body of Christ, broken for you. This is the blood of Christ, shed for you." Our community said these words in faith; we received the elements by faith. What else could we do? In that moment, all the violent, racist evidence from our society pointed to the futility of our little multiracial community. The very act of receiving the body and blood of Jesus was evidence either of our delusion or, perhaps, of our mustard seed–sized faith that the cross of Jesus was more powerful than this world's hatred. I believe it was the latter and that, in that terrible and tender moment, our community was being discipled.

Our practiced habit of coming to the table steadied us in our grief and confusion. The Lord met us not simply in the elements but in and through one another as we were pulled once again to the One who is our center.

■ ■ ■

Our first reimagined discipleship practice is Holy Communion. Christians have different ways of observing Holy Communion, including how often it is received. But whether it is the weekly or monthly practice of a church, we hold in common the belief that Communion is to be revered, that its frequency is a mark of its importance. Different theological frameworks undergird how we think about this meal, but Christians share the highest regard for the body and blood of our Savior.

What makes Holy Communion so essential to Christians across time and place is the belief that without the grace to which this sacrament points, there would be no church. Not only did Jesus command his disciples to observe this meal, but its very essence captures our story: guilty of sin, we have been spared by the shed blood of Jesus the Christ, incorporated into his very body by his atoning and victorious death and resurrection. At table we remember and participate in the righteousness of God as accomplished by his Son. At table we are grounded within the divine drama: Christ has died! Christ has risen! Christ will come again!

At table, we participate in the grace that reconciles us with our God. But there is another side to our eucharistic celebration that we will highlight as we reimagine Holy Communion as a practice to disciple white Christians away from our segregation. Theologian Theresa F.

Latini draws our attention to this other characteristic by highlighting the Greek word *koinonia*, or "fellowship." She writes, "The church's *koinonia* with Christ and the *koinonia* among its members cannot be severed from each other. Participation in both is the twofold vocation of every Christian."[1] The fellowship won for us with the Father by his Son is one that is also expressed in our fellowship with one another.

This twofold vocation is seen clearly in passages like 1 John 1:3: "We proclaim to you what we have seen and heard, so that you also may have fellowship with us. And our fellowship is with the Father and with his Son, Jesus Christ." We are forever relationally intertwined with our Lord and his people. As theologian Simon Chan writes, "Through the Eucharist the Spirit actualizes the communion between Christ and his body and between the members of his body. Communion is at the heart of the Eucharist."[2] Once we see the essential nature of our fellowship with one another at table, we can begin to appreciate the significance of how this sacrament is framed communally throughout the New Testament. So before considering its formational potential, let's look at four ways the Lord's Supper grounds us within the fellowship of believers.

■ ■ ■

1. SERVICE

At the very first Communion meal, an argument broke out among Jesus' disciples. The dispute began immediately after Jesus served the cup. And what was the argument about? Hierarchy. They were fighting about which of them was the greatest. But Jesus would have none of their positional bickering: "For who is greater, the one who is at the table or the one who serves? Is it not the one who is at the table? But I am among you as one who serves" (Luke 22:27). Here Jesus pointed to one of the essential attributes of his ministry, that despite his identity as God's Son and Israel's Messiah, he came as a servant. It's a characteristic that extended to the table where he served his quarreling disciples.

Though the Gospel of John leaves out the details of the Last Supper, in this version Jesus' service is even more visible. Here he seems to demean himself by taking on the role of the foot-washer, an act so debased that Peter recoils in horror. Again, Jesus pointed to his actions at table as prescriptive for his disciples: "I have set you an example that you should do as I have done for you" (John 13:15). At table, Jesus expects his disciples to demonstrate the sacrificial service that his last meal with them foreshadows. There was to be no pecking order, no hint of the status or power imbalance that was then so typical in the Roman Empire—or so characteristic of the racial hierarchy of our society today.

The servant nature of Holy Communion is no less radical for us than it was for Jesus' first disciples, even though we are adept at blunting its sharpest edges. We spiritualize fellowship so that we think about our fellow believers as our equals, but only in invisible ways which generally don't require any material sacrifice. Or we limit fellowship to individual relationships, imagining only those within our immediate and, most likely, racially homogenous community as the people we are called to serve. When we do venture beyond our immediate communities, our service can be paternalistic, as we assume to know how best to serve those who never asked for our help in the first place.

The early church would have a hard time recognizing this tepid view of fellowship. In Acts we learn that the believers "devoted themselves to the apostles' teaching and to fellowship, to the breaking of bread and to prayer" (Acts 2:42). The subsequent verses show this to be a material fellowship, a relational oneness that could be seen and that challenged the empire's deeply held hierarchical assumptions. The abundance of the Lord's Supper overflowed to the material provisions given to those who were in need. The twofold vocation was essential to these believers: fellowship with Jesus was inseparable from fellowship with one another, and both were physically expressed at table.

One reason we overlook the upending of hierarchies first exhibited at the Lord's Supper is that white Christianity has segregated itself from the evidence of our racial hierarchies. Certainly there are socioeconomic and class differences within white communities, but the structural hierarchies of race and the economic disparities inherent in them are largely invisible to us. It's not necessarily that white Christians have ignored the call to serve across racial disparities; we've simply ignored the disparities altogether.

Though our segregation may keep us from the servant nature of the Lord's Supper, it is no excuse. Think, for example, of Paul castigating the church in Corinth for the way they had accepted cultural hierarchies as the norm, even as they came to the table. "So then, when you come together, it is not the Lord's Supper you eat, for when you are eating, some of you go ahead with your own private suppers. As a result, one person remains hungry and another gets drunk" (1 Corinthians 11:20-21). Apparently the Corinthian Christians brought the distinctions of class with them to the table. Rather than reorienting their fellowship around the presence of the Servant-King, they allowed their culture's hierarchies to dictate how they treated one another. Paul warns that accepting these hierarchies means that the meal the Corinthian church shared could no longer be accurately thought of as Holy Communion. It's a warning we should heed. So strong is Jesus' call to servanthood at table that anything other risks becoming a meaningless religious ritual.

2. SUBMISSION

Theologian and pastor David Fitch writes that when Jesus inaugurated the Lord's Supper, "the issue of mutual submission rushes to the forefront."[3] Mutual submission is closely related to servanthood, but I think it's important to sound this note clearly and distinctly for white Christians.

The "dividing wall of hostility" that Jesus destroyed between Jew and Gentile was not simply a matter of relational separation. It was a matter of religious and social hierarchy (Ephesians 2:14). In Acts 15, we see that the early church faced the important question of whether being culturally Jewish was somehow more acceptable to God. Did the new Gentile Christians have to become something else before becoming disciples of Jesus? Time and again, the New Testament answer is a resounding *no!* The vision instead is one of mutual submission, in which both Jew and Gentile submit to their Lord Jesus and, thus, to one another.

When my wife and I were in the process of adopting our first son, we had to take transracial adoption classes. As white parents who planned on adopting a child of color, we needed to consider some of the important cultural and societal realities that our child and family

would face. One of the activities left a strong impression on me. We
were each given a clear jar and a bag of colorful beads; each color represented a different race or ethnicity. The facilitator then asked the
class—mostly comprising white adoptive parents—a list of questions
about the racial and ethnic diversity of our personal lives. For example,
What is the predominant race or ethnicity of your neighborhood? Or,
What race or ethnicity is most represented in the music you listen to?
For each answer, we were to choose the bead that represented our
answer and drop it into the jar.

In this visible way, most of us came to see how culturally white our
lives were. This led to a challenging conversation about the decisions we
could make so that our lives would be more hospitable to our adopted
children. It was a powerful exercise, but there were some specific questions that especially grabbed my attention. What race or ethnicity is
your pastor? Your doctor? Your boss? These were questions about the
people who had authority in our lives. Who, in other words, was I sub-
mitted to? Sadly, like most white people, there were very few people of
color who had genuine authority in my life.

Fitch writes that the Lord's Supper "leads us into submission to Jesus
Christ as Lord." This central submission then "spreads out into mutual
submission to one another. And a new social order is birthed out of this,
which is nothing less than his kingdom."[4] In a society whose job market
remains relatively stratified by race, for example, many white people
have never had a reason to submit to a coworker of color. Given the
segregation of white Christianity, the same is likely true for most white
Christians. Because racial whiteness has as its basic function materially
privileging white people over others, the eucharistic call to submission
is incredibly important to highlight, again and again. Because our racialized society disciples us not just toward segregation but into assumptions of supremacy as well, white Christians need to feel our
mutual submission when we come to the table.

3. REFLECTION

In some Communion liturgies the congregation will be asked to examine their hearts before receiving the sacraments, the language being

borrowed from 1 Corinthians 11:28: "Everyone ought to examine them-selves before they eat of the bread and drink from the cup." The current of individualism that runs so deeply through white Christianity leads us to think of this important part of the Lord's Supper in highly indi-vidualistic terms. So, for example, we might recall an unacknowledged sin that can be confessed before coming to the table. This is all well and good, but the context for Paul's admonition to examine ourselves is one in which class divisions and disparities had not been dismantled by the church. He is urging the church to consider how they, corporately, had succumbed to their society's divisive hierarchies.

The call to examine ourselves can include unconfessed individual sin, but we understand it more fully when we see it as an invitation to the entire community. Though it may initially seem strange, Holy Com-munion is a natural time for us to reflect on how racial discipleship has deformed our desires and assumptions. When we sanitize the world's injustices and bring them with us to the table, we are, according to Paul, "guilty of sinning against the body and blood of the Lord" (1 Corin-thians 11:27). It's a sober warning, and it reveals just how deeply rooted the Lord's Supper is within the fellowship of believers.

4. FEASTING

As Jesus inaugurated the Lord's Supper with his disciples, he pointed ahead to the day when his kingdom would be realized (Luke 22:29-30). Yes, this meal reminds us of the sacrifice made by Jesus for our salvation, but it also draws our imaginations into the future when the kingdom of God is established in its fullness at Christ's glorious return. Here we can think of the wedding banquet portrayed in Revelation: "Then I heard what sounded like a great multitude, like the roar of rushing waters and like loud peals of thunder, shouting: 'Hallelujah! For our Lord God Almighty reigns'" (Revelation 19:6). And, of course, this is a feast that reflects the immense cultural diversity of the kingdom of God. The mul-titude is "from every nation, tribe, people and language" (Revelation 7:9).

Like so much of Christian worship, the Lord's Supper anchors us in the already-but-not-yet of kingdom life. We remember Christ's fin-ished sacrifice on the cross even as we anticipate his victorious return.

We receive Christ's body and blood in faith, both for what has already been accomplished and for what it prefigures, a day when nothing will hinder the nations, tribes, and peoples from gathering *together* around the throne "and before the Lamb" (Revelation 7:9).

In the liturgy of many denominations, right before serving the sacraments the officiant says, "The gifts of God for the people of God—take them in remembrance that Christ died for you, and feed on him in your hearts by faith, with thanksgiving." If we're paying attention, we will again see our twofold vocation. At the feast, we take Christ into our hearts as the sufficient sacrifice for our sins, and we are turned outward to the others who have joined us at the feast. We take our place at the feast within the diverse multitude of worshipers, praising God alongside our sisters and brothers.

The Lord's Supper extends that future feast into our present. The manner in which we observe table fellowship today should, at the very least, hint at the future feast that has been promised to us. As we break bread and pour wine, we step away from our society's segregated hierarchies and embody instead the new people we are through Jesus Christ.

■ ■ ■

In these four characteristics of Holy Communion—service, submission, reflection, and feasting—we see that it must be understood within the context of our fellowship with one another and how the New Testament places this fellowship within the context of cultural and ethnic disparities. As we turn to reimagining how the Lord's Supper can begin discipling white Christians away from segregation, we need to expand the scope of our fellowship. If the segregation that characterizes white Christianity is neither natural nor normal but is an expression of our society's deforming racial discipleship, then we must begin to imagine our Christian fellowship as including those we have historically excluded. If the Lord's Supper is rooted in Christian fellowship with one another, and if racial discipleship has segregated us from one another, then reimagining the Lord's Supper means recognizing that our fellowship *must* extend beyond our segregation. How might that look?

Given the individualism that is endemic to much of white Christianity, it will be important to regularly teach the communal nature of the Lord's Supper. If we are to be shaped toward solidarity by the Communion meal, this note will need to be sounded more clearly by preachers and teachers. Otherwise we will miss the comprehensive reality that in the "bread and wine Christ is manifested as the Victor over sin and death, the Conqueror over the devil and all that is rebellious against God."[5]

We should think of teaching not only as transferring information but also as inviting white Christians to engage with the questions and confusion raised by these theological nuances. Small groups, for example, can be an ideal setting to discuss what mutual submission across lines of racial and ethnic segregation could look like for the members of these groups. A campus ministry might host similar conversations, perhaps inviting members of an African-American or Asian-American ministry to speak to their experiences of the cultural exclusivity of white Christianity. These smaller, discussion-oriented spaces provide the structure for difficult conversations, vulnerable questions, and, eventually, creative new possibilities.

From this expanded understanding of our Christian fellowship, we can now turn to some ways to reimagine the practice of Holy Communion that lead to solidarity.

LAMENT

As the Lord's Supper becomes more intentionally rooted in the fellowship of the believers, the gaps between what white Christians profess and what we practice will become increasingly evident. White Christians will begin to wonder why our table fellowship is such a faint reflection of the future heavenly feast. Or, to use another example, as we examine ourselves before coming to the table, we might question why we have been content to leave our society's hierarchies undisturbed within our fellowship. For many white Christians, Holy Communion is a time of relief as we remember the sufficient work of Christ's death and resurrection. But now, the Communion table will become a source of growing unease for segregated Christians.

While this could be a catalyst to retreat to more individualistic expressions of the Lord's Supper, it can also be fashioned into lament. By including the Scripture's language of lament in our Communion liturgy, we invite white Christians to sit with our turmoil and to interpret it as an invitation from the Holy Spirit.

Because most communion liturgies include a corporate confession of sin, it will not take much effort to add some additional language that gives voice to a community's lament. A stanza from a lament psalm such as Psalm 79:8 can give white Christians the words and images we need for our lamentation: "Do not hold against us the sins of past generations; may your mercy come quickly to meet us, for we are in desperate need." By pointedly identifying segregation and racial injustice as incompatible with the church's fellowship, believers can both grieve over how we have misrepresented the kingdom of God and repent for the personal actions that have contributed to these sinful realities. Because biblical lament is never passive, the invitation to the table is a regular assurance of God's grace that extends through our sin while calling us to live more fully by that same grace into the reconciled kingdom of God.

SERVE

I once had an older African-American man as a ministry supervisor. As he neared retirement, he would sometimes tell me stories of serving in our predominantly white denomination. One of these involved a trip to visit a church in a small midwestern town. In his telling, my supervisor couldn't remember seeing another person of color in town the entire duration of his stay. That Sunday a ministry leader in the church he was visiting invited him to serve Communion with him. The lay leader held the plate with the bread, and my supervisor held the cup. As the members came to the front, tearing small pieces from the loaf before dipping them in the cup, my friend noticed that one man purposefully avoided looking at him. When he made it to the front, this white man took some bread and then, immediately, ate it. Abruptly he turned his back on the only black person in the church, intentionally avoiding my supervisor and the cup he held.

While most of us can hardly imagine such a blatant display of racism today, the fact remains that most white Christians have rarely, if ever, been served the Lord's Supper from someone who does not share our race. The opportunity to serve and receive the Lord's Supper within a racially diverse fellowship can be a powerfully formative experience. However, the logic of white Christianity generally precludes this sort of reconciling table fellowship. To live into this fellowship, a white Christian community needs to intentionally seek it out. For some this could look like a yearly combined worship service. I know of some congregations that come together for a community-wide Good Friday service. Perhaps a white church could partner with another church for a service project in their neighborhood that would begin or end by celebrating the Lord's Supper.

We must also acknowledge that it's possible to have an occasional experience with racial diversity that makes no lasting impact on a white ministry. As we've seen, when white churches attempt to become racially diverse, they usually end up perpetuating white culture. That is, rather than being changed themselves, white Christians expect others to change. But the service of the Lord's Supper that I'm suggesting here fits within a larger and longer-term scope of discipleship. So we are not looking to these cross-racial experiences of table fellowship as evidence of racial reconciliation but as the slow re-formation of our desires and assumptions. The difference may seem small, but it is important if we are to engage in diverse table fellowship, even occasionally, in a manner that honors our Christian family.

COLLABORATE

Many churches receive a special offering after celebrating the Holy Communion. Sometimes these gifts are for needs within the church; other times they may be sent to another country to address a particular opportunity. As we begin to think about Communion as an expression of our fellowship with other believers, this special offering could raise possibilities for solidarity.

To imagine how this might look, let's consider church planting. Either through their denominations or other networks, many white

churches help start new churches. Congregations give generously so
that a new church can be planted in a neighborhood or town that
seems to need one. As a church planter myself, I am very thankful for
the generosity and enthusiasm that churches like these show for
starting new congregations. But I've also noticed something troubling
about how white Christians sometimes go about starting them. Rather
than reaching out to the other churches—often churches of color—
that are already faithfully ministering in an area, we simply set up
church and then announce that the gospel has finally arrived to this
neighborhood or town. I am exaggerating, but only slightly. The not-
so-subtle message, whether intentional or not, is that white Christianity carries the true message of the gospel. I once suggested to a white
church planter who was considering starting a church in a black neighborhood that he partner with the churches in that neighborhood.
Doing so, though, would require him to expand his very white theological boundaries. This was a bridge too far, and he admitted, "I just
love my theology *so* much."

But what if, rather than starting a church in a different neighborhood, a white church were first to purposefully develop a relationship with, for example, an immigrant congregation in that same
neighborhood? So, rather than organizing to start a church to reach
immigrants—which would likely perpetuate the assumptions of white
culture—this church would learn to see the faithful ministry that is
already happening among immigrants, led by other recent immigrants.
And then, to bring this back to Holy Communion, what if the Communion offering was tied directly to the ministry opportunities and
needs faced by that immigrant congregation? On a regular basis the
white church would hear updates and testimonies from their sisters and
brothers. Rather than giving to an abstraction, the generosity provoked
by Communion would be directed to the embodied fellowship which
transcends racial segregation. And because the offering is taken as part
of the Lord's Supper, the possibility of paternalism and feelings of
superiority can be mitigated by connecting the financial gifts with our
own profound spiritual needs.

EAT

The boundary between the Lord's Supper and a community potluck was less distinct for the early church than it is for us. The description of the early church in Acts 2 shows the believers devoted to breaking bread and prayers as well as eating together in their homes "with glad and sincere hearts" (Acts 2:42-47). Our church celebrates Holy Communion on the first Sunday of the month. After the service, we roll in a bunch of round tables and everyone who can sticks around for a potluck. Some people grab chicken or pizza on the way to church. Others come with Crock-Pots to plug in or casserole dishes to warm up. It's one of my favorite things that we do together. Sometimes I'll stand at a distance, marveling at the racial diversity around the tables—people laughing and catching up, children sneaking cookies from the dessert table. There's something holy about these potluck lunches.

Latini writes that churches can "explore how their meals together are more than physical sustenance (though they are that, of course). Their table fellowship can be approached as mutual feeding analogous to Christ's feeding of us in the Eucharist. Accordingly, their meals would take on the flavor of spiritual as well as physical nourishment."[6] She is thinking particularly of small groups when she notes the Communion-like possibilities of shared meals. While large-group, racially diverse potlucks might not be sustainable for most churches, smaller group meals are relatively easy to organize.

There are many ways meals can be shared across lines of segregation. Many white churches host other congregations in their buildings. I know of one church that hosts an African-American church and multiple immigrant congregations. Each weekend in this church facility you will find incredible cultural diversity. Yet typically, there is very little engagement between congregations in a setting such as this. But what if a quarterly or monthly time was set aside for all of the congregations to gather together over a potluck dinner? There would be plenty of awkward moments; language could be a complicating factor in some communities. But over time, these extensions of the Lord's Supper could have a powerful impact on white Christians whose relationships most likely would otherwise remain racially isolated.

I know of two churches—one black, the other white—whose intentional relationship began by hosting regular meals for each community's leaders. Over food and through growing friendship, these churches discerned an ever-closer relationship that was eventually expressed in service to the community and times of combined worship. At the risk of being repetitive, we need to remember that our goal is not to pursue racial diversity as the answer to segregation. However, the increasingly diverse fellowship that began over potluck dinners is one expression of how the Lord's Supper as a discipleship practice can begin forming white Christians toward solidarity with their diverse family in Christ.

■ ■ ■

By embracing our twofold vocation of fellowship—with Christ and one another—we can begin to imagine how the practice of celebrating Holy Communion can begin to orient us toward solidarity with the body of Christ. By grounding the Lord's Supper deeply in the fellowship of believers across lines of racial segregation, this sacred meal will only grow in its power to transform our desires and to fulfill them.

CHAPTER FIVE

PRACTICING KINGDOM PREACHING

Does a chapter about preaching belong in a book about *communal* discipleship practices? Ten years or so ago I wouldn't have thought so. My view of preaching and teaching then shared much in common with the way pastor and professor of preaching Frank A. Thomas describes how many of us think about communication in general. We assume that when a person "wants to communicate, one engages in a cerebral process that takes ideas, wraps them in words and symbols, and transmits them to another person. The other person decodes the message according to similar cerebral processes, and comprehends the message."[1] Most seasoned preachers, though, wouldn't agree that such a clinical, transaction-like process is what actually takes place during a sermon or a teaching. But I don't think it's a stretch to assume that when we come to a preaching moment, most white Christians take a rather individualistic and mostly passive view of what is happening. We don't think of preaching as something we experience communally so much as an opportunity to receive something for our personal edification and formation. White preaching is often directed solely to congregation members' minds, with the assumption that right personal thinking or believing will lead to individually changed lives. As much as we esteem the preached gospel, it isn't something most of us consider a practice in which we participate together.

So before we turn to some ways preaching and teaching can be re-imagined as a discipleship practice that orients white Christians toward solidarity, we need to see how gospel proclamation is a communal practice. And then, because we are interested specifically in the disci-pleship of white Christians, we need to dig more deeply into the nature of societal privilege, which shapes white identity. Once we've grappled with these two things, we will see more clearly how one of the most common aspects of a Christian community's life together can disciple us toward the reconciled kingdom of God.

■ ■ ■

I began noticing how preaching can function as a discipleship practice for a community when I was exposed to black churches and became aware of the different ways a sermon often functions in these communities. Thomas writes that the "nature and purpose of African American preaching is to help people *experience the assurance of grace* (the good news) that is the gospel of Jesus the Christ."[2] It's the word *experience* in his definition that is important for us. As Michael Emerson points out in his study of multiracial congregations, the differences between white culture and black culture impact how Christians think about something as essential as preaching. Whereas white culture typ-ically divides intellect from emotions, African-American "culture does not split mind and body. The two components are viewed as important and intertwined, and it would be artificial to separate them and rank one over the other."[3] With this difference in mind, we can better see why the experience of preaching in many black churches is so im-portant; it is a way for whole persons to participate together with the proclaimed Word of God.

But there is more to our different ways of experiencing the preached gospel than broad cultural distinctions. Importantly, for black Chris-tians the experience of gathering for worship has historically been a communal one. Throughout the week these women and men live in a racialized society in which something as arbitrary as skin color has set them apart for systemic disenfranchisement and personal encounters with racism. But on Sunday morning, black families and individuals gather for corporate worship. The history of the African-American church in this country marks these congregations as sanctuaries from the attacks on their personhood suffered each week. That is, as black Christians come to worship, they often do so as a community that has been called out, kept safe by the providence of God for another week.

When the preacher steps into the pulpit each Sunday morning, the congregation anticipates a communal experience of the assurance of the gospel. Those in the pews are not a random assortment of individuals but a cohesive people who desire to be shaped together by the proclamation of God's word. The call and response, applause, frequent standing, and other embodied interactions with a sermon that are common to varying degrees in many black churches are all evidence of a people being discipled *together* as the Word is preached. In the white churches of my childhood, following Sunday worship we often asked each other what we remembered from the sermon, anything we would individually reflect on in the week to come. In contrast, I sometimes hear African-American friends say of a recent service, "We had some *church* today!" The language is corporate and experiential, a statement about what a community under the preached Word has encountered.

Obviously there is no such thing as a monolithic black church, just as there are countless variations within white Christianity. But in the same way that white Christianity holds in common the assumptions we unearthed in Part One, so too are there shared themes, such as the communal experience of preaching, within many black churches. And it is this communal experience that is important for us to see if we are to understand how gospel proclamation can be reimagined as a discipleship practice for solidarity.

Two things are necessary if white churches and ministries are to realize the formational potential of the pulpit. The first, following our African-American sisters and brothers as well as other Christians of color, is to see the congregation composed of fully embodied people. As important as it is to preach thoughtfully and engage the intellect, preaching that only does this fails to respect the whole person, created in the image of God to respond to God with our entire beings. Second, like many Christians of color, white Christians will need to see ourselves corporately. Coming to see ourselves as a people who have been formed (and deformed) communally will allow white Christians to see the Word of God, faithfully and regularly proclaimed, as an indispensable aspect of our discipleship.

Once a white church begins to see preaching as a corporate discipleship practice, other small things can be done to increase community engagement with the sermon. I've known some churches that invite people to stay around after the sermon for a time of discussion with the preacher. Including space for questions and comments invites church members to see themselves as integral parts of the preached gospel. It might seem like a small thing, but in churches where the norm is to sit quietly throughout the entire sermon, a preacher who occasionally asks for an amen is reminding his congregation that they are more than disembodied minds. Some churches have the tradition of occasional testimony services. In these settings, I have seen how one person's story of God's provision highlights the commonalities that run through the community, both in terms of the struggles being faced along with God's grace to meet us together in our trials.

Small things like these over time can help a congregation re-envision its engagement with a sermon. But, after coming to see preaching itself as a communal discipleship practice, the most important step a white Christian community must take is to acknowledge its white identity. Preaching as a communal practice only makes sense to a people who understand their commonalities, even if these are related to the pains and injustices of racial privilege and prejudice. It is to this challenge that we now turn.

■ ■ ■

White people, simply by dint of our race, are granted a measure of privilege by our racialized society. For white people, the process of seeing ourselves *as* a people very importantly involves acknowledging this unearned privilege.

In my experience, bringing up this topic is a great way to stop a conversation in its tracks. Time and again, well-meaning white people who dispute the notion that they are privileged have told me that they, too, have experienced hardship in their lives. Some of us were raised with the belief that anyone can get ahead in our society if they're willing to work hard enough; the notion that anyone has been given an advantage because of their race would be laughable if it weren't so offensive.

Ken Wytsma, founder of The Justice Conference, offers a helpful response to these pushbacks. He writes, "White privilege doesn't mean your life isn't hard. It means that if you are a person of color, simply by virtue of that, your life might be harder." He continues, "White privilege means that even if you're the unluckiest white person born in the United States, you were still born into a fortunate race."[4] This is essential for us to understand. Regardless of the personal setbacks and struggles we've each known—including structural prejudices against women and poor people, for example—racial whiteness still grants white people a measure of advantage that differs for people of color.

By now it should be plain that any privilege associated with whiteness originates from the construction of race. There is nothing inherently better about my white skin, only what that skin has come to symbolize in a racialized world. As professor and author Michael Eric Dyson writes to white people, "Whiteness is an advantage and privilege because you have made it so, not because the universe demands it."[5] In the United States, "constructions of race have never been morally neutral. Racial construction processes have always meant and continue to mean today that persons with phenotypes marking them as 'white' receive better treatment, greater social access, and more institutional benefits than those with phenotypes that mark them 'of color.'"[6]

Here's one way to think about this: rather than privilege following from the reality of race, the reality of race follows from the pursuit of privilege. In other words, to think carefully about race—especially whiteness—we must also grapple with the malicious pursuit of power and privilege. Without reckoning with this ugly reality, white Christians will never account for the ways our society has misshaped us.

Another way to grapple with my privilege is acknowledging the obvious difference race makes in certain circumstances. Years ago I was driving through a predominantly white town with my wife next to me and an African-American friend in the back seat. I must have been in a hurry to get to our after-church lunch because the police officer who pulled me over clocked my car going well over the speed limit. After running my license and registration, he walked up to my window, bent down, and spoke those sweet words: "I'm letting you go with a warning." As we drove away my friend was barely able to contain his incredulity when he asked, "A warning? He gave you a warning?" He explained that he'd never been given a warning by a police officer and that he'd never heard of anyone being given a warning. I think he was only being slightly sarcastic when he said something like, "I didn't even know police were *allowed* to give warnings."

My friend's experience is not unique. Though they are no more likely to break traffic laws than white drivers, black and Hispanic drivers are disproportionately more likely to be stopped by the police. They are also more likely to be searched, ticketed, and arrested.[7]

As a white man, I experience racial privilege in these sorts of inter-personal encounters, during which I am often given the benefit of the doubt simply—and absurdly—because of my race. But given our claim that privilege is intertwined with the construction of race, we should also expect to find instances of it at more systemic levels. The housing disparities that we considered in the first chapter are one such example. This history of racist policies that excluded people of color from fed-erally backed mortgages and rapidly appreciating suburban develop-ments resulted in today's staggering wealth gap between white and black people. A racialized society that is built on white supremacist social structures will inevitably benefit those it was built to privilege. Conversely, that same society will marginalize, exploit, and oppress those who are without racial privilege.

As a Christian, it is even more important to acknowledge the spir-itual nature of racial privilege. Professor of preaching Charles Campbell believes that Christians should think of racism and privilege as part of the rebellious principalities and powers that we find in New Testament passages such as in Ephesians, where Paul writes that the Father "raised Christ from the dead and seated him at his right hand in the heavenly realms, far above all rule and authority, power and dominion, and every name that is invoked, not only in the present age but also in the one to come" (Ephesians 1:20-21).[8] Seeing racial advantage as a spiritual power opposed to the will of God helps us to see that its destructive impact is "not just limited to the oppressed. . . . The privilege that comes to white people can destroy their spirit in a different way."[9] Though Christ's victory at Calvary ensures these earthly powers' ultimate submission to his Lordship, in this in-between time we still suffer and battle their rebellious and destructive agendas. Because our task in this chapter is to reimagine gospel proclamation as a practice for racially privileged people, let's look at two of the ways the rebellious power of privilege has left its stain on our spirits.

■ ■ ■

The first impact of racial privilege on white people is how it fosters emotional immaturity. Dyson describes what this immaturity feels like to a black man like himself when he writes, "We are forced to be gentle with you, which is another way of saying we are forced to lie to you. We must let you down easy, the powerful partner in a fraught relationship. Your feelings get hurt when we tell you that you're white, and that your whiteness makes a difference in how you're treated."[10] He is getting at the responses so many of us have when topics like racism, white privilege, and, especially, white supremacist social structures are brought to our attention. Too many times I have watched a white person explain to people of color why their understanding (actually, their lived experience) about any of these topics is incorrect. Other times the response looks less rational; emotions like anger or shame shut down the conversation. Rather than drawing from an emotional reserve of courage and humility, many white people in these moments use our words and feelings to direct the attention elsewhere.

I've come to believe that a large part of this emotional immaturity is connected to how white privilege breeds forgetfulness. This is not surprising given the origins of racial whiteness. To become white, our ancestors had to forget who they were. Language, culture, and the particularities of a place long inhabited were encumbrances to the American Dream, a dream that could only be attained by those deemed to be white.

This forgetfulness extends to the many ways our racialized society, and our active roles within it, have harmed others. One of the characteristics of societal privilege is not having to remember how our assumptions and actions have inflicted harm on others. In my wife's hometown, for example, there is a roadside marker commemorating one of the city fathers. On it he is described as a good Christian and citizen, a man whose charitable giving bought one church's property and whose taxable income funded the town's coffers. What is left off—notable only if you know the history—is that this apparently upstanding Christian man was also one of the state's largest slaveholders. Conveniently forgotten in this official narrative is the fact that his great wealth and subsequent benevolence were a direct result of his enslaving and exploiting women and men of African descent.

Maybe this seems like an extreme example, but the experience of white privilege is littered with stories like these, past and present. This forgetfulness results in another aspect of our emotional immaturity, which is a belief in our innocence in matters of race. Because we have forgotten the ways our privilege is built upon the marginalization and exploitation of others, we are able to see ourselves as blameless when it comes to society's racial ills. It's not that we're oblivious to all expressions of racism; in fact, many white people are willing to criticize overt racists. But by scapegoating the obvious racists, the rest of us can rest in our blamelessness. This supposed innocence conceals our complicity with a racialized society, making it all but impossible for white people who have not acknowledged our privilege to do much about racism other than defend and deflect.

In 1962 James Baldwin wrote an essay, "My Dungeon Shook," in the form of a letter to his nephew. In it, he candidly addressed the perceived innocence of white America.

This innocent country set you down in a ghetto in which, in fact, it intended you should perish. Let me spell out precisely what I mean by that, for the heart of the matter is here, and the root of my dispute with my country. You were born where you were born and faced the future that you faced because you were black and

for no other reason. The limits of your ambition were, thus, expected
to be set forever. You were born into a society which spelled out
with brutal clarity, and in as many ways as possible, that you were
a worthless human being.[11]

Baldwin is pointing out—in a manner that ought to make us
squirm—the absurdity of white innocence given the devastating foundations of whiteness. "But it is not permissible that the authors of dev-
astation should also be innocent," he writes. "It is the innocence which
constitutes the crime."[12] Here again we see how race—and, in Baldwin's
warning to his nephew, the pain of racism—should be understood as
proceeding from the pursuit of powerful privilege. And though this
painful truth has been all but impossible for most of white Christianity
to confess, our forgetfulness and perceived innocence makes it none the
less real. Writes Campbell, "To the extent that the church enjoys the
privileges of this order, the church, including the pulpit, is complicit in
this violence."[13]

Some African-American churches celebrate a special Juneteenth
worship service each summer. This service remembers the date June 19,
1865, when enslaved people in Texas finally learned about the Emanci-
pation Proclamation, more than two years after it was issued by President Lincoln. The celebration carries significant theological overtones,
a picture of God's salvation spoken into a sinful world that does not yet
acknowledge King Jesus. There's no reason that white churches, bound
to our African-American family in Christ, could not also honor this
unique expression of God's liberating presence—yet sadly, most white
Christians haven't even heard of Juneteenth. Instead of joining our
sisters and brothers in these sorts of remembrances, we're isolated in
our forgetfulness and supposed innocence.

There is a great irony for white Christians about our forgetfulness
and innocence: neither is biblical. Time and again God urges his
people to *remember.* They are not to forget his faithfulness, and neither
are they to forget their own sinfulness. Piles of stones and the names
of places were all supposed to stir questions about days gone by, memories of desperate needs and miraculous provisions. From the Old

Testament through the New, God's people are to remember that salvation is not dependent on our righteousness but on the grace of God alone. It is not our innocence that saves us but God's grace applied to our guilt. A sign of a mature faith is a strong memory about my sinful need and God's abundant provision. But these elements are what white privilege diminishes.

■ ■ ■

In addition to emotional immaturity, the second impact of racial privilege is how it hinders white people from experiencing community. Perhaps this is obvious given the segregation experienced by white Christianity, but it's essential to notice how unacknowledged privilege disrupts the flesh-and-blood community for which we were created. The narrative of racial difference is, at its core, a lie about humanity; it claims that some of us are more fully human than are others. Racial privilege, particularly when it is unrecognized or denied, embraces this false narrative as though it were real. It breathes legitimacy into the offensive racial lie.

Over the years, I've reached the disappointing conclusion that most white people, including Christians, simply do not expect our communities—churches, neighborhoods, friend groups, and so on—to include people of color. For most of us, it's fine if there is some racial diversity within our communities, but it's not something we're anticipating or working toward. And when our communities *do* include people of color, we expect them to conform to the norms and assumptions of whiteness. Our racial privilege has led us to *imagine* our communities as being white.

The vision of the kingdom of God that we find in the New Testament is one in which women and men who had been divided by their society's hierarchies were each pulled toward Christ. Yet because our imaginations have been stunted by our privilege, many white Christians do not even want this sort of reconciled community. Instead, our privilege leaves us susceptible to the deceptions of our racialized society. "All too often," writes Campbell, "privileged Christians approach marginalized people as 'problems.' And people in power usually deal with problems by taking control and fixing them."[14] This has often been my experience. White Christians who see people of color as problems deserving their benevolence will give generously to projects and ministries designed to help them. But invite those same Christians into relationships of shared power or, even less likely, submission to Christians of color, and the response is far less enthusiastic.

An even more malevolent stereotype of people of color, fueled by racial privilege, has to do with our fear. Quoting Ida B. Wells, Eddie Glaude writes, "The world has accepted the story that the Negro is a monster, which the southern white man has painted him. And, today the Christian world feels, that while lynching is a crime, . . . it cannot by word or deed, extend sympathy or help to a race of outlaws."[15] Although Wells wrote these words over one hundred years ago, the sentiment remains strong.

As I worked on this chapter, a high-profile case involving a white police officer who killed a young black man in Chicago was coming to its end. Despite the fact that the officer shot Laquan McDonald sixteen times and that the video showed him emptying his gun into the young man even as he was walking away and falling to the ground, the defense painted the victim in dehumanizing terms. In the closing arguments, the officer's lawyers told the jury, "Think about a monster movie when the victim is hiding in the bush . . . there is not much danger. But when that monster suddenly stops and turns and looks right at the victim in the bush, that is when the music starts to play."[16] Thankfully the jury did not succumb to this old and destructive trope but, in a way, the defense was simply verbalizing the ugly assumptions that animate racial privilege. "White fear is the danger," writes Glaude. "Not black people."[17]

However damaging racial privilege is to white people, however much it has warped our imaginations and stained our spirits, it is exponentially more destructive to people of color. For white people, privilege fosters emotional immaturity and interrupts the possibility of reconciled community. For people of color, the hazards are far more visceral, the risks that our privilege will destroy lives too great to ignore. This is what is at stake as we consider the potential of gospel proclamation to disciple privileged people. Confessing and confronting racial privilege is an essential stop on the road from segregation to solidarity.

There are many ways gospel proclamation could be reimagined as a discipleship practice; we'll look at four.

■ ■ ■

1. BE SPECIFIC

First, in majority white settings, community members should regularly reflect on who they are. That is, they can reflect on the fact that their community is white. Such an approach resonates with the language of Scripture.

In the Old Testament we find that the people of God regularly considered the particularities of their identity. At times this process is joyful; other times they must confess their affliction. The prophets are especially good at directing God's message in the most specific of terms. They speak blessings and warnings to particular nations and kings. When they confront Israel, they do not do so generally; their words are rooted in time and place, peppered with the names of people, nations, and events familiar to the community. The New Testament epistles are another example of communities who are learning to apply the gospel to the nuances of their distinct circumstances. The authors of these letters address their teaching and admonitions to unique people and their situations. Gospel proclamation that speaks directly to the privilege of whiteness is simply following the pattern of particularity that we find in Scripture.

During a church conference a few years ago, I was invited to join a racially diverse panel to address some of the racial injustices and divisions that were then in the news. The conference was largely white, so I addressed my comments directly to the white attendees. After the panel I was surprised by how many people of color wanted to talk with me. What impacted most of them was not any great wisdom or insight that I shared, but simply that I spoke to white Christians. I remember one older Latina woman who shook her head, almost in disbelief, as she told me that she'd never in her life heard white Christians specifically addressed from the stage of this conference. The response by the white attendees was somewhat different; most of them were unaccustomed to having the distinctions of our race being noted so precisely.

The notable thing about this reaction is that, in my experience, Christians of color regularly reflect on their racial, ethnic, or cultural particularities. An immigrant church considers the struggles of being seen as perpetual foreigners by the dominant society, or the challenges of raising children who have increasingly more in common with that society. A youth ministry of color thinks about its students and the struggles they face because of their race. The pastor of a black church I recently visited reminded his people during the sermon of the faithfulness of previous generations of African-American Christians who, despite great oppression, built churches and other community institutions that nurtured their neighborhood to this day.

One of the privileges of whiteness is thinking of ourselves only in the most general terms. Unlike the examples in Scripture or the practices of Christians of color, white Christians rarely address our particularities. But by regularly acknowledging the reality of race, gospel proclamation can begin helping white Christians see our privilege. This can be as simple as noting the demographics of our communities and recalling the differences racial privilege makes in the lives of white Christians. These small nudges will help white Christians begin to see the practical difference race makes in everyone's lives, including our own—those of us who have been conditioned not to think about ourselves in racial terms.

2. EDUCATE

One of the regular arguments against talking about racial injustice (and other so-called social issues) from the pulpit is that it distracts from the gospel. According to this line of thought, anything other than the simple and straightforward preaching and teaching of the Bible is a capitulation to the ideologies of our society. The problem with this is that it assumes a simplistic understanding of communication. As Frank Thomas noted at the beginning of this chapter, a preacher does not simply transmit disembodied knowledge to the minds of the congregation. Effective communicators understand that they must take seriously the contexts and circumstances that have shaped their hearers. When we miss this, we greatly diminish the effectiveness of our preaching and teaching.

Again, white Christianity can learn a lot about this from Christians of color. Because these sisters and brothers understand that fundamental aspects of their humanity are neither seen nor valued within a racialized society, they realize that gospel proclamation must include an educational component. Native American Christians, for example, have long had to remind their children that their culture is not inferior to the dominant one that has done such damage to their communities. In response to plans by white denominations and government institutions to assimilate young Native Americans into white culture, these communities have had to find ways to teach their children about their history and culture. In this manner, the gospel is applied to their specific moments of suffering and resilience.

In a nation built on the narrative of racial difference, African-American churches have also found it essential to prioritize cultural education. If the definition of blackness was left to the racialized society, African Americans would be left with a wholly inaccurate view of their humanity. Left unchallenged, our nation's racial hierarchy will consistently threaten black Christians' perception of the image of God with which they, like all of us, have been endowed. So it is common to find sprinkled throughout many a black preacher's sermons those historical examples of black resilience, stories of previous generations whose faith shaped lives of courage and resistance to oppression. The communities that sit under such preaching will find that the gospel addresses not some general representation of themselves but their very specific situations.

Within white Christian communities, education should also play a significant discipleship role. By reflecting on the construction of whiteness or on the unearned privileges it bestows upon us, white Christians will begin to see the segregating effects of race. The goal is not to turn sermons into seminars about white privilege, but rather to begin including educational elements that help white Christians see ourselves and our situation more accurately. Doing so does nothing to diminish the key tenets of our faith. Rather, our beliefs are directly applied to our lived discipleship and the barriers that have kept us from reflecting the biblical vision of the kingdom of God. The goal is to show how the gospel speaks directly to our circumstances, no matter how deeply they have been obscured within a racialized society.

3. REMEMBER

Another way for gospel proclamation to serve as a discipleship practice that shapes white Christians toward solidarity is to resist the forgetfulness of white privilege. Because our Christian faith so strongly depends on our willingness to remember our need for salvation and God's saving response through Jesus, remembering is an essential component whenever the gospel is proclaimed. By including the specific nature and impact of racial privilege in what we remember, the preached gospel can begin addressing these specific sins and wounds.

Not long ago I was invited to address a gathering of mostly white Christian leaders. Many of these women and men came from small towns that are largely white, and many of them wondered if they had a role in addressing racial injustice.[18] I began my talk by referring to one of my favorite novels, *Gilead*, by Marilynne Robinson. The novel takes the form of letters from the aging pastor John Ames to his young son, in a small Iowa town in the 1950s. Rev. Ames is a third-generation preacher. While his own father was a pacifist, the reader learns that Rev. Ames's grandfather moved from Maine to the Kansas frontier before the Civil War in order to join the abolitionist fight against slavery. The fictional town of Gilead, like some real towns throughout the Midwest, was founded to help enslaved people escape and to change the balance of power in the nation so that future states admitted to the Union would be free. These were the frontlines in the battle for freedom and racial justice. But by the time Ames writes to his son, this history has long passed. The town has settled into a contented apathy, its roots in the great battle against slavery almost entirely forgotten.

Ames writes that, before his abolitionist grandfather died, he left Gilead for the scenes of his former battles in Kansas.

He was terribly lonely, no doubt about it. I think that was a big part of his running off to Kansas. That and the fire at the Negro church. It wasn't a big fire—someone heaped brush against the back wall and put a match to it, and someone else saw the smoke and put the flames out with a shovel. (The Negro church used to be where the soda fountain is now, though I hear that's going out of business. That church sold up some years ago, and what was left of the congregation moved to Chicago. By then it was down to three or four families. The pastor came by with a sack of plants he'd dug up from around the front steps, mainly lilies. He thought I might want them, and they're still there along the front of our church. I should tell the deacons where they came from, so they'll know they have some significance and they'll save them when the building comes down. I didn't know the Negro pastor well myself, but he said his father knew my grandfather. He told me they were sorry to leave, because this town had once meant a great deal to them.)[19]

The black pastor and his congregation remembered the Gilead of the past. But now, during the era of Jim Crow laws and lynchings, they no longer felt welcomed. Their church, the symbol of their faith and freedom, suffered an arsonist's attack. They had to leave. And what is it that Ames remembered most about this time? The flowers. In contrast to his grandfather, he has accepted the assumptions of his day. It's not that he's a rabid racist; he seems to remember the black church fondly. Instead, like the rest of the town, he views the fire and the black community's subsequent departure as a benign fact of history. By the time he writes to his son, not a single black person remains in Gilead, and nothing about this troubles the abolitionist's grandson.

I shared this with the audience as a way to show the importance of remembering. The white leaders, many from towns similar to the fictional Gilead, began to wonder what racial histories from their communities had been forgotten. After all, what we take as being normal, inevitable, or the results of benign choices are often the results of malicious decisions made long ago. By recalling these stories, we invite white Christians to see our present circumstances differently and less passively. The characters and battles in our history can serve as an effective antidote to the forgetfulness of privilege. Remembering can lead white Christians to join the rest of the body of Christ in resisting the forces of forgetfulness.

4. FIND COMMONALITY

One of my ministry colleagues serves a vibrant congregation in a small midwestern city. On the rare occasion when we get to share a meal together, I am always struck by how much my mostly black, urban neighborhood shares in common with his mostly white, rural city. In both locations there are strong community bonds going back generations. Both communities experience disparaging portrayals in the media— mine having to do with racial stereotypes, his related to assumptions about the perceived backwardness of rural America. Both have known economic disinvestment and the scourge of illicit and addictive drugs. In both of these communities, high school sports are weekly highlights of community pride and involvement. The list could go on.

Yet the specter of racial difference means that these two communities rarely find common cause with each other. Instead, my friend's community, because they have almost no meaningful contact with people of color, is likely to assume that they have nothing to learn from those with whom they share so much in common. These assumptions are then brought to church, where they are typically left unchallenged.

But when gospel proclamation begins connecting the relationships that racial privilege has distracted us from, white Christians can begin seeing the larger body of Christ to which we belong. There will be practical benefits to finding this sort of common cause. As an example, imagine if rural churches invited leaders from urban congregations to speak about ministering to communities that feel increasingly disenfranchised, a reality that seems new to many white communities but that has long been the experience of some communities of color. Beyond the practical benefits, when gospel preaching and teaching move white Christians to find common cause with the body of Christ, we are moved one step further from our segregation, one step closer to solidarity.

CHAPTER SIX

PRACTICING
SUBVERSIVE LITURGIES

It might seem strange to include a chapter about the Sunday liturgy in a book that is in one sense all about liturgy.[1] We have seen how we are daily discipled by the practices, or liturgies, of our racialized society. In these pages we are attempting to take seriously this liturgical deformation that orients our desires away from the kingdom of God and leaves us content in our racial segregation. The practices we are reimagining, which aim our habits and desires toward solidarity with the body of Christ, are also liturgical. "Christian worship," writes James K. A. Smith, "functions as a counter-formation to the mis-formation of secular liturgies into which we are 'thrown' from an early age."[2]

But despite the liturgical foundations on which this entire book sits, thinking specifically about how the Sunday liturgy—the specific forms of worship—functions when a church gathers will prove fruitful in our attempt to reimagine some of the discipleship practices that are already active in most of our congregations.

I admit to some nervousness on writing about liturgy. Most of my experience has been of the low-church variety, with little overt awareness of the forms that undergird our worship. If you were to worship with our church, you would not find an order of service in the bulletin. Most of our services do not have scripted responsive readings or prayers, though they are a part of our celebration of Holy Communion. But if you were to look closely, the forms of our worship would become apparent and hopefully resonate with the liturgies of many other churches. We will get to those common liturgical elements, but for now I simply want to acknowledge that every church service is liturgical. That is, when a church gathers for worship, there are forms that guide how we worship, and those forms are full of potential to disciple us toward the kingdom of God. It is the specific, common elements of the Sunday liturgy that we will consider in this chapter.

In some of our traditions those forms are a visible and honored aspect of our congregational life; for others, the liturgy functions more like a current, barely visible and only occasionally acknowledged, yet doing the important work of aiming our worship. Pastor, author, and multicultural worship leader Sandra Van Opstal recognizes that while "not all worship traditions speak in terms of liturgy, all include some form of repeated structure, whether formal or informal."[3] Wherever we find ourselves on this liturgical spectrum, the common elements of the Sunday liturgy can help reach our goal of discipling white Christians away from racial injustice and segregation. Before we look at how this could happen, we will broadly consider how the church has thought about what liturgy is and how it impacts us as we worship.

■ ■ ■

When we talk about the church's liturgy, we are talking about worship that is embodied. It is the *form* of how the congregation, in harmony with the historic and global church, expresses its worship of the triune God. Dating from the fifth century, the phrase *lex orandi est lex credendi* ("the rule of prayer is the rule of belief") points to this cohesive relationship between what Christians believe and how we express our belief in worship. There is a sense in which belief shapes the forms of worship, but equally important is how the forms nurture belief. Of course, this is an idea that we've already grappled with through these pages; now we are simply seeing how it resonates with the church's weekly liturgy.

The form of our worship matters, writes Smith, "not because of any traditionalism or conservative preservation of the status quo, but precisely because . . . there is a logic to a practice that is unarticulated but nonetheless has a coherent 'sense' about it. Form matters because it is the form of worship that tells the Story."[4] If people were primarily thinking or even believing beings, this would be less important. The forms of corporate worship would matter far less than the basic information that is communicated. But, as Augustine helped us see, we are desiring and loving beings. As important as is biblical truth plainly communicated, our discipleship must account for *how* we receive and respond to that truth. The liturgy of Christian worship provides the structures that allow for more than the transfer of knowledge; it invites whole persons into embodied expressions of worship. The liturgy honors our humanity and forms us in the story of God.

At its most basic—and most profound—the church's liturgy is anchored in Word and Sacrament. The proclamation of the gospel and the celebration of Holy Communion are central to the rhythm of worship, and I've dedicated individual chapters to both of these. Without these there is no church, either in constitution or expression. But while the liturgy is anchored by the proclaimed Word and the celebrated feast, there have always been other elements that allow the church to enter God's story each time we gather for worship. It is these other elements of worship that we will explore later in this chapter.

While considering the Sunday liturgy, it is important to state clearly that we do not mean a certain *style* of worship. The common forms of Christian worship, expressed across culture and history, allow for an incredibly diverse array of styles. Given our focus on racial injustice and segregation, this is important to highlight. Thinking about liturgy as embodied worship in harmony with the forms of worship throughout church history allows us to see how liturgy operates in a Pentecostal church composed of Latino and Latina immigrants, in an African-American Baptist church, or in an Asian-American university prayer ministry. Each of these and a host of others are examples of how the liturgy shapes worshipers toward the kingdom of God. There is no such thing as worship that exists outside of cultural and ethnic perspectives.

■ ■ ■

To reimagine the Sunday liturgy as a discipleship practice that leads to solidarity, it's helpful to consider how the church has thought about what liturgy *does*. In other words, how does the form of worship shape the worshipers? For our purposes, I want to suggest that the liturgy shapes our orientation to God, time, community, and mission. Unpacking these will help us see the untapped potential of the liturgy to serve as a counter-formation to our racialized society.

Joseph Cardinal Ratzinger, who became Pope Benedict XVI, writes that the uniqueness of the church's liturgy "lies precisely in the fact that God himself is acting and that we are drawn into that action of God. Everything else is, therefore, secondary."[5] In worship, it is always God who moves; we, the people of God, respond to what God has done, is doing, and will do.

We know this, of course, but corporate worship can easily begin not with the fact of God but with our own concerns and interests. We come to worship formed by a culture of individualism and consumerism—beginning with anything *other* than ourselves and our perceived needs requires the intentionality of the Sunday liturgy. Biblical worship redirects our attention away from ourselves and to the God whose mighty acts seize our imaginations. This divine orientation is embedded in the church's liturgy, helping the congregation to resist our culturally fueled self-centeredness.

By turning us toward God, the liturgy also disrupts our natural experience of time. By nature, we are forgetful creatures. God's command to the Israelites in Deuteronomy 4:23 is one we can't hear often enough: "Be careful not to forget the covenant of the LORD your God that he made with you." This instruction is so important that different forms of it are found repeatedly throughout Scripture. But we still forget. We time-bound creatures are prone to forget God's faithfulness, not to mention the righteous future won by Christ's death and resurrection. In worship, we are freed from our myopic view of the present moment and ushered into an experience of God's redemptive movement throughout the ages. In worship, the past and future are connected and held together beyond the urgencies of the present moment. Liturgy, then, resists our tendency to reduce everything to our current experience. Rather, the forms of worship cause us to remember and to anticipate.

The worshiper's orientation toward the rest of the congregation is also shaped by the liturgy. We come to worship as a collection of individuals, shaped culturally to think of church as something we choose. Yet despite the strong pull of our culture, individualizing the work of God is not inevitable. As Ratzinger notes, "All our singing is a singing and praying with the great liturgy that spans the whole of creation."[6] In contrast to worship experiences that begin by attempting to meet the individual's needs, the liturgy invites individuals to join the communion of saints who for generations have found their place within the community of God's people. As we move through the elements of the Sunday liturgy, we join the generations across time and place who have made similar weekly journeys toward the heart of God.

Finally, the liturgy has a missional orientation. Though it is common for churches to prioritize missions in a variety of ways, the implicit message of many contemporary worship services is that missions is for someone else—the preacher or missionaries. In contrast, the liturgy as *lex orandi est lex credendi* expects the congregation to participate in God's story—past, present, and future. It is not enough to hear the story or even to believe it; the liturgy gives us the form to enact our parts in God's story. And, as Ratzinger notes, this participation extends from the worship service into the rest of our lives: "The true liturgical action is the deed of God, and for that very reason the liturgy of faith always reaches beyond the cultic act into everyday life, which must itself become 'liturgical,' a service for the transformation of the world."[7] Far from retreating from the world, the liturgy orients us toward the world as God's ambassadors.

■ ■ ■

With this basic understanding of what liturgy is and what it does, we can identify some of the distinct aspects of the Sunday liturgy. These practices fit within the shape of the liturgy, anchored by Word and Sacrament, which gather the church from the world before sending us back as ambassadors of reconciliation. The church has generally envisioned a fourfold structure for the Sunday liturgy: the entrance, the proclamation of the Word, Holy Communion, and dismissal. By creatively imagining this structure as a meal hosted for friends, Van Opstal helps us see how the liturgy can be contextualized across styles and traditions.

Gathering: You warmly welcome people at the door.

Word: You engage deep conversation at home and a sermon at church.

Table: You share a meal.

Sending: You part with hugs at home and a benediction at church.[8]

In the remainder of the chapter, we'll explore some of the distinct aspects of the Sunday liturgy following this structure with an eye to how these can be reimagined as desire-orienting practices that lead white Christians away from our racial segregation and injustice.

As an aside, I realize some readers may worry that I am tinkering with something that ought to be left alone. As we've noted, the basic shape of the liturgy is ancient, and my attempt to reimagine some elements could be perceived as irreverent or as a novelty for its own sake. To such potential objections I can only appeal to the conviction that the forms of our worship express what we believe about God and our relationship to God. As theologian Simon Chan cautions, "If the liturgy only makes us feel good and never challenges us, perhaps the liturgy is not shaping us but we are simply making use of it for our own ends."[9]

Given how powerfully the practices of our racialized society operate on us, we can reasonably expect that the Sunday liturgy will challenge us deeply, at the uncomfortable levels of our assumptions and imaginations. Forms of worship that orient our desires toward the kingdom of God and solidarity with the body of Christ will inevitably disturb and disrupt those of us who've been malformed by practices infected by the narrative of racial difference. To the extent that the Sunday liturgy leaves white Christians comfortable in our racial segregation, it's reasonable to wonder what must shift in order to allow these ancient forms to move us once again more deeply into God's story.

ENTRANCE

The *call to worship* is one of my favorite parts of any worship service, and I have to contain my mild disappointment each Sunday when so many congregants stroll in after it's over. There is something mystical about this moment: as individuals we are called from the necessary responsibilities and pleasures of our everyday lives to enact something else, the church. We are *called* to worship as an expression of who we already are, even if, throughout the week, we've lost sight of our fundamental identity as the people of God.

During a recent sabbatical I worshiped with a neighborhood congregation pastored by a close friend. This African-American Pentecostal congregation begins each service crying out to God in prayer, led by a layperson at the podium. In prayer these women and men are called back to what is most true in the universe: that there is a God, that this God rescued them, and that their identities and futures are secure in his hands.

Intrinsic to being called *to* worship is the fact that we are also called *away* from something else. While a white church may have some sense of this calling away, the failure of white Christianity to identify racial segregation and injustice as forces opposed to the kingdom of God means we don't imagine them as what we must leave behind. I'd hazard to guess that when coming to worship most white Christians are not consciously aware of being called away from the racial hierarchies that have been at work on our imaginations all week. By identifying racism among the other sins from which we are being called away, white Christians can experience the liturgy as genuinely countercultural, an invitation to God's story which challenges the warping contours of our society's narrative.

Depending on the tradition, the *greeting*, or the sign of reconciliation and peace, might happen during the entrance or after the sermon but almost always before Holy Communion. Oftentimes the pastor will say to the congregation, "The Lord be with you," to which the people respond, "And also with you." Having been called to worship, we are now welcomed. Because the liturgy points to God's story, it is God who welcomes us. The grace of Jesus is manifestly expressed in that we are not strangers or interlopers in God's house but friends whose presence is desired.

The expression of this welcome, just as the rest of the liturgy, must be embodied so there is a time for the congregation to greet one another with the peace of Christ. As a reflection of Jesus' command to be reconciled in Matthew 5:23-24, we are given an opportunity to extend hospitality to one another before coming to the Lord's Supper. We welcome one another, confessing and forgiving anything that would keep us from coming to the table as friends.

Given the segregated nature of white Christianity, most white Christians will not regularly have the chance to intentionally extend the greeting across lines of racial segregation. In those churches that do have some amount of diversity, the greeting can be a time when the worldly separations and sins are acknowledged. That is, the church can be called to greet one another in a manner that does not ignore the sins of personal racism and systemic racial injustice but rather urges us to welcome one another, through the Holy Spirit's power, in the face of these sins. There is no redemptive future in the tendency among many white Christians to ignore the complicated and disturbing realties associated with race. But there is hope once these are acknowledged and we discover that the grace of Jesus is more than enough to call us together in worship.

The challenge is greater for those churches that have little or no racial or ethnic diversity. In these contexts it will be enough to remind the church of the great diversity within God's family that is, often at the same moment, extending God's welcome to one another in a nearby sanctuary. During those occasional times when a white church is brought into worship with those of other races or ethnicities—such as a combined worship service on a special occasion—the greeting can be explained and extended in a way that allows the congregation to experience God's reconciliation in a manner that typically remains theoretical within a segregated church.

Though *congregational singing* happens throughout the liturgy, songs of adoration are generally part of the entrance, the sung truth about God preparing our hearts to hear the gospel proclaimed. Early in the life of our multiracial church, we held a Sunday evening meeting in a member's basement, where we began reflecting on our experiences in our racially diverse community. One white woman not long out of college described how much she struggled with one of the choruses we occasionally sang. This particular song, "I Need You to Survive," comes from the black church tradition and focuses on the experiential reality of our interdependence as Christians. Our African-American worship leader would exhort us to look one another in the eye as we sang these words about our need for each other as members of Christ's body. This young woman confessed she disliked the song so much that she would escape to the restroom each time we began to sing it.

But all of this changed for her the Sunday our worship leader explained the personal significance of the song. She described how she had countless experiences of the church being the very presence of Christ to her in the midst of a society that often does not see or value her. When she sang about needing other members of the church—"I need you, you need me. We're all a part of God's body"—she was singing a deep theological reflection about her lived reality, testifying to the ways God had been tangibly present to her through his people. After she told us this story, the white woman smiled and said, "I won't leave when we sing that song anymore."

Singing is an especially embodied part of the liturgy. The songs and hymns of the church are ripe for pointing to the great and beautiful diversity within the body of Christ. The discomfort expressed by the young woman about that song was less about its words than about *how* it was sung. Perhaps she had grown up in a tradition that looked mostly at a hymnbook or a video screen during congregational singing. Being urged to physically acknowledge and sing to other members of the congregation was far outside her comfort zone. But once she understood why this way of singing mattered to other members of her community, she could begin opening herself up to the song and, more importantly, to the women and men she was bound to in Christ.

As we sing, we harmonize with the church down the street or across the tracks whose allegiance to Jesus we share, even if our tempos and tunes differ. A white church can choose to include songs that fall outside its cultural tradition, stylistic preference, or even the English language. Of course, singing in a different language does not make a church multicultural, but done with humility, these decisions can remind the white congregation that their cultural or ecclesiological preferences are not neutral. There will be awkward moments: mispronunciations and out-of-rhythm clapping, for example. But when led carefully, these sung experiences will remind a white congregation that there are others within their Christian family singing that same song of adoration to God, often at that very hour and in close proximity, but from a very different vantage point.

In recent years we have seen Latino/a migrants and immigrants maligned and scapegoated by pundits and politicians. While our particular church has only a few Latino and Latina members, we have found it to be a powerful experience to occasionally sing in Spanish. We join with sisters and brothers who praise God from exceedingly difficult circumstances in our heavily accented voices. The experience of singing in their language moves us, however slightly, closer to lived solidarity.

Another part of the entrance is the *confession and assurance of pardon.* Many Protestant traditions will use language similar to that found in the Anglican Book of Common Prayer:

> *Most merciful God,*
> *we confess that we have sinned against thee*
> *in thought, word, and deed,*
> *by what we have done,*
> *and by what we have left undone.*
> *We have not loved thee with our whole heart;*
> *we have not loved our neighbors as ourselves.*
> *We are truly sorry and we humbly repent.*
> *For the sake of thy Son Jesus Christ,*
> *have mercy on us and forgive us;*
> *that we may delight in thy will,*
> *and walk in thy ways,*
> *to the glory of thy Name. Amen.*[10]

I hope it is apparent how this regular part of the liturgy might disciple white Christians away from segregation. To begin with, the corporate language strikes at the heart of our individualistic instincts. And while we can think about the language of the confession as covering our corporate status as sinners, we can also reimagine it to identify the sins shared by our race. Our complicity with racial segregation and injustice is a sin against God—in thought, word, and deed. The neighbors whom we have not loved as ourselves include our neighbors of color, whose painful experiences often prop up our privileges, experiences we have often ignored or denied. Our sins of omission include leaving our racialized society undisturbed. Our sins of commission include the ways we have leveraged our privilege for our own benefit.

Equally important for white Christians is what follows after our shared confession. In the words of absolution we hear the gospel applied to the specificity of our sin. In my tradition, the pastor proclaims, "If we confess our sins, God is faithful and just to forgive us our sins and cleanse us from all unrighteousness. May Almighty God have mercy on us, forgive us all our sins through our Lord Jesus Christ, strengthen us in all goodness, and by the power of the Holy Spirit keep us in eternal life. Amen." In a society in which being called a racist is about the worst, most shaming label that can be applied to a person, these words of assurance remind white Christians that our hope comes not from pretending to have escaped the influence of a racialized society but, through the power of the gospel, in confessing our sinful complicity with it.

PROCLAMATION OF THE WORD

We've dedicated a chapter to *preaching*, so I won't add much more. But it's worth noticing the importance of the sermon within the flow of the Sunday liturgy. We've seen how the sermon can be specific about the nature of racial whiteness, how it can include educational elements that help white Christians make connections between our race and faith, how white Christians can be called to remember what racial whiteness works to make us forget, and how the preacher can help the congregation see what it has in common with Christian communities of color. Preachers who have reimagined the possibilities of the sermon will come to this moment in the liturgy with new expectations. As they stand before their congregation, resting on the authority of Scripture, they will see a people in need of tender but courageous instruction. Following the entrance to worship, these preachers will look for ways to bring the Bible to bear on particular experiences and their white congregants. These experiences may have to do with how racial privilege works to isolate us from others or, as we've seen, how white people have been formed to see ourselves as largely innocent of the sins of racism.

Preachers who have carefully exegeted these sorts of racial and cultural complexities will be able to precisely apply the authority of Scripture to their people.

The *prayers of the people* follow the sermon in many traditions. These prayers typically include four areas: needs in the church, civil authorities and salvation of the world, those facing difficulties, and the local community.[11] The language in these prayers is always corporate; it is the church as a whole that presents itself in petition to God.

A couple of times each year, my family attends an ecumenical Taizé prayer service in a neighboring town. The service is simple, with repetitive choruses that are easily learned no matter what tradition a person is used to. The service is also interactive, with candles lifted high as we sing before placing them at the altar. But it is the prayers of the people that often seem to be the most interactive element of the service. As voices are raised with specific petitions in the ornate sanctuary, my mind and heart are drawn to consider and pray for situations that might not have otherwise crossed my mind: those suffering homelessness, the loss of a child, the salvation of a spouse, wisdom for elected officials, unity in the church.

Following the sermon and preceding Holy Communion, the prayers of the people in a white church can likewise include specific requests for churches of color with whom the church is in relationship. This portion of the liturgy can also be one of the most responsive to current events; when another traumatic example of racial injustice takes place in public view, the church can identify it specifically in prayer as they cry out for comfort and justice.

As in our discussion about Holy Communion, the prayers of the people will also become a natural place for a white church to voice its lament to God. Rather than allowing the newfound awareness of their complicity with racial injustice and the suffering of people of color to devolve into debilitating shame, corporate prayer gives voice to difficult and confusing emotions. In prayer, a white church finds that racial injustice is not primarily partisan—as much of our media would have us believe—but ecclesial. We pray from the growing and painful awareness that the family members to whom we are related in Christ have suffered the weight of our privilege. This part of the liturgy leads away from shame; we are redirected back to God's story as active and responsive participants whose honest lament leads us closer to reconciliation.

HOLY COMMUNION

As with the proclamation of the Word, there is little to add that hasn't been covered in a previous chapter. Yet it's important to reiterate how profoundly essential the Lord's Supper is to white Christians who are being discipled toward solidarity with their family in Christ. Feeding on Christ "in your hearts by faith, with thanksgiving" is an experiential necessity for those who are being made aware of their complicity with racial injustice. Our hunger and thirst for the Eucharist becomes palpable as we grow more aware of the ancient sins of racism and supremacy and how thoroughly they have infected our discipleship.

The *offering* is often associated with the Lord's Supper, usually directly preceding or following it. Smith writes that "the liturgical practice of the offering indicates that Christian worship—which is a foretaste of the new creation—embodies a new economy, an alternative economy."[12] More than an act of charity or giving from our disposable income, the offering reveals "a reconfiguration of distribution and consumption" within the kingdom of God.[13]

The nature of racial privilege in the United States extends far beyond the realm of personal benefit. Racism and segregation function not only to separate those of different races but to actively disenfranchise people of color, especially African Americans and Native Americans, though anyone who is not white is also susceptible. Author Ta-Nehisi Coates points to this long, ugly history.

America is literally unimaginable without plundered labour shackled to plundered land, without the organizing principle of whiteness as citizenship, without the culture crafted by the plundered, and without that culture itself being plundered.

White dependency on slavery extended from the economic to the social, and the rights of whites were largely seen as dependent on the degradation of blacks. "White men," wrote Mississippi senator and eventual president of the Confederacy Jefferson Davis, "have an equality resulting from a presence of a lower caste, which cannot exist were white men to fill the position here occupied by the servile race."[14]

White Christians in this country cannot help but to materially benefit from this legacy of bloody plunder. This isn't to say that there are not many white people who struggle financially, only that no white people are poor because of their race.

Whether acknowledged or not, we bring this sordid economic history with us when we gather to worship. Yet the offering reveals the alternative economy of the kingdom of God. This is an economy of costly grace wherein we can tell the truth even about topics our culture considers taboo, such as the origins of our wealth or the ways we are complicit in someone else's poverty.

When the offering is received, a white church can be reminded that the New Testament vision is of a reconciled community who "shared everything they had" so that "there were no needy persons among them" (Acts 4:32, 34). In this church, wealthy members were willing to sell land and homes for the proceeds to be "distributed to anyone who had need" (Acts 4:35). How might a white church that is waking up to the racial origins of economic inequity follow the early church's example? How might church budgets be reimagined? How might gracious generosity be redefined? Imagine the financial metrics that could be employed to allow these Christians to joyfully proclaim, "There are no needy persons among us, the people of God reconciled across segregation and divisions!"

DISMISSAL

We come finally to the end of the liturgy and to two parts that pass quickly but are latent with potential. First is the *benediction*, the final blessing of the worshipers. Appropriately, as the entire liturgy points beyond ourselves to the God who welcomes us, in these words of blessing the people are reminded again of the source of our hope and salvation. The most common benediction, from Numbers, is illustrative.

"The LORD bless you and keep you; the LORD make his face shine upon you, and be gracious to you; the LORD lift up his countenance upon you, and give you peace" (Numbers 6:24-26 NKJV). Though the liturgy has asked us to look at the parts of our sinful humanity we'd rather avoid, it's in the benediction, before we are sent back to the world, that we hear the tender assurances of our Lord.

A community of white Christians discipled toward solidarity with the body of Christ will be thirsty for these words of blessing. For a people who have long been intertwined with the deceptions of race, the benediction is no mere formality but an anchor in deep and convulsing waters. Before we reenter the deceptive narratives of our racialized society, we must hear that our gracious God will keep us, will hold us, will protect us. As the world we had assumed to know so well grows shaky under the weight of new and difficult knowledge, we will reach our arms high and wide for the benediction. Sometimes the weight of racial injustice will feel crushing. Other times, as we awaken to our sinful complicity, we will be strongly tempted to hide in shame. But then we are embraced in blessing. We are almost literally lifted to our feet by the incredible announcement that the Lord has not turned away his loving gaze. So, rather than pulling back or returning to our previous ignorance, we find the strength to move forward in the grace of God.

And then we are *sent* into the world, disciples called to make new disciples of Jesus. But now, having been shaped by the liturgy together, we emerge with new eyes to discern the world more truthfully. In a real sense the liturgy has given us eyes to see what we'd previously missed. We see, for example, that as we are called to worship as a people, we are now sent not as isolated individuals but as a community. And, regardless of the racial segregation to which we've long been accustomed, we are now coming to understand our inextricable relationship to the entire body of Christ.

■ ■ ■

In the black churches I've worshiped with, it's common for the exodus to emerge as a major theme in the liturgy, no matter what forms it takes. The story of God's liberating power extended to his people in Egyptian captivity is rehearsed and celebrated by these churches—as it is throughout much of the Old Testament. The congregation is pointed back to God's mighty acts in the past. In worship, they remember that God has acted in this world for his glory and their good. This theme is powerfully illustrated in the words of the spiritual "Bound for Canaan Land":

> *Although you see me going so*
> *I'm bound for Canaan land*
> *I have trials here below*
> *I'm bound for Canaan land*

More than an escapist vision of heaven, these joyful words anticipate a future in which God's salvation is expressed in the physical escape to freedom. It is an expression of faith that God will once again act within history for his people's well-being.

The remembering-anticipating posture that is natural in so many black churches is what white churches must grow into if we are to disciple people toward solidarity. By reimagining aspects of the Sunday liturgy, we will move intentionally in this direction.

CHAPTER SEVEN

PRACTICING CHILDREN'S MINISTRY OF RECONCILIATION

ONE OF THE FIRST QUESTIONS we ask during the racial reconciliation workshops I assist with is this: When did you first realize that race matters? In mixed-race pairs, we then have the participants share their responses and the stories behind them.

While the specifics always vary, there is one trend that never seems to change. For the people of color, especially the black participants, the awareness of the significance of race comes very early in life. This is usually due to an unforgettable encounter with racism or because parents or other adults explained why, even as children, it was important to pay attention to how race operates in America. For these participants, their consciousness about race came in their early elementary school years. It was not an option *not* to know about race and its real-life impacts.

In marked contrast, I've yet to hear a white person share a racial awareness timeline anything like that of the participants of color. In fact, if my anecdotal observations match reality, most white people don't intentionally think about race until early adulthood. In these cases it is usually the exposure to new information—a black studies class in college, for example, or a history professor who is more honest about

America's legacy of racism than are most high school curricula, or racially diverse friends—that opens their eyes to the power of race. Even after these new experiences and the growing awareness about race to which they can lead, the white participants in our workshops quickly figure out just how little time they've spent thinking, worrying, or even caring about race compared with their partners of color. This pattern is certainly true in my own life as well.

In his essay "Down at the Cross," James Baldwin reflected on his teenage years growing up in Harlem in the 1930s and 40s. In it he recalls what it felt like growing up in a country in which race meant far more than benign difference. Race, the young Baldwin came to understand, was fundamentally about power, about making white people superior to the black people who populated his neighborhood. This malevolent power differential is at the heart of race and, as Baldwin came to see, long "before the Negro child perceives this difference, and even longer before he understands it, he has begun to react to it, he has begun to be controlled by it."[1]

We need to hear Baldwin's sobering reflection as we consider how our children engage with discipleship practices of solidarity. We will spend most of our time in this chapter thinking about the impact of race on white children and how their assumptions and imaginations can be reoriented toward the kingdom of God. But we cannot forget that race reserves its most deadly force for children of color. All children are susceptible to exploitation and oppression, but in our racialized society children of color are especially vulnerable. For example, I have seen firsthand how mass incarceration and gun violence touch the lives of many of the African-American children in our communities in Chicago. It is the rare hand that does not go up when I ask a group of young people whether they know someone in prison, or if they've personally been impacted by a shooting. It's no wonder that the adults of color in our workshops had to understand the force of race so early on.

But the fact that white children do not have to reflect on race does not leave them unscathed by it. The deformation of white people's assumptions and desires begins early in life. Therefore, any attempt to lead a white Christian community away from racial injustice and segregation must include our children. Specifically, there are two reasons why our white Christian children must grapple with race early on. The first has to do with our goal in these pages: solidarity with the racially diverse body of Christ. It's always a grievous moment when the white workshop participants realize how much longer their African-American partners have been grappling with race. As they begin waking up to the parallel—and segregated—lives they have led, the uneasiness is palpable. How could something so important to these sisters and brothers in Christ have been invisible to them? In *Raising White Kids*, professor Jennifer Harvey notes that as children of color are developing an understanding of the many ways race matters personally and systemically, "white children are left alone to internalize racism, or taught to actively ignore race."[2]

The other reason we must include our children in these discipleship practices has to do with their own spiritual formation. Our children are born into the smog of our racialized society. Whether or not they recognize it or their parents point it out, these children are born into the historical wound of racial whiteness that, as Wendell Berry says about his own life, was "prepared centuries ago to come alive in me at my birth like a hereditary disease, and to be augmented and deepened by my life."[3] Too often, rather than helping them see through the deceptive smog to the truth, we leave our white children's imaginations to be corrupted by the narrative of racial difference. And when we abandon our children to the deceptions of our racialized society, they "will observe racial disparities for themselves and explain them by presuming something must be wrong with people of color."[4]

Pastoring a multiracial church means I have many conversations about race with our members. One of the distressing trends I've noticed with some of our white members, usually young adults, is how their new racial awareness can destabilize their faith. As they form meaningful cross-racial friendships and participate in ministries of racial reconciliation, these women and men come to see how much they missed, or were shielded from, in their youth. They discover that racial divisions in the church are not benign reflections of cultural preference but the bitter fruit of racial superiority and privilege. Through the testimonies of their new friends of color they discover a Christianity that was never compelled to separate personal salvation from social justice.

All of these discoveries lead them to reflect on the faith of their childhoods with critical eyes and probing questions: What else wasn't I told? Can I trust the motives of those who nurtured me in the faith? How much of my faith has not been tainted by a complicity with racial injustice and segregation? Thankfully, these difficult questions often lead to a deeper, more robust expression of Christian faith now in solidarity with the body of Christ. But more often than I want to admit, I have watched these younger white Christians walk away from the faith, the deceptions of the past seemingly too much to overcome.

In the same way we would expect Christian discipleship to impact our children in other important areas of their lives—sexuality, money, work, and so on—we should also anticipate their attitudes and desires about racial justice and reconciliation to look different from those of their non-Christian peers. Such a distinctive way of living beginning early in life would bode well as these young Christians leave the security of home and become more aware of the racially unjust world.

■ ■ ■

As Eddie Glaude puts it, racial habits not only shape "how we interact with people of different racial backgrounds, they also guide how we think about and value groups collectively. And like many habits, they are formed when we are young."[5] As Baldwin remembered, these habits were being molded in his own life at an early age, but the same is true for white children. In large part, this simply has to do with how children see and categorize the world. Professor Phyllis Katz ran a well-known study in which she observed six-month-old babies staring longer at photos of people whose race differed from that of their parents. When these children were three and were shown photos of other children and asked which ones they would choose as friends, 86 percent of the white children chose photos of other white children. When they were six years old, the children were asked to organize a pile of drawings of different people. While some chose to sort the pile by gender, most chose to do so by race.[6]

What are we to make of how early children—all children, but here
we are especially thinking about white children—see racial difference?
Well, on a basic, innocent level our children are simply observing the
world around them. When they see and sort by race, they are doing
what kids do. But by now we are aware that these neutral observations
will quickly become tainted by the narrative of racial difference. For
example, as Harvey points out, white children

> see how many places and spaces have only one racial group present
> in them (and which racial groups are present in what kinds of
> places). They notice who holds which jobs at supermarkets, res-
> taurants, schools, or doctors' offices. They then generalize what
> they see to draw specific (false) conclusions about why it would
> be that doctors are white and custodians are Latino/a, or why no
> Black people go to church, and on and on.[7]

Without a conscious awareness of the roots of inequity, our children's
imaginations and assumptions will be shaped by the simplistic and deceptive narratives of a racialized society.

As any new parent understands, children are constantly observing
and interpreting the world and, as these same parents soberly realize,
it's the parents themselves who are most closely watched. These observations lead inevitably to imitation. It's not that white parents and
caregivers must be explicitly and obviously racist in order to pass on
racial bias to our children. The pervasive nature of the racialized smog
means that our silence about race will be interpreted as approval of the
way things are.

This dynamic was especially apparent in a recent article I read about
how white parents who view themselves as politically and socially progressive often reinforce the narrative of racial difference to their
children. The author points out the tension experienced by these
parents. "Many parents, in fact, expressed a desire to have their ideals
and parenting choices align. In spite of that sentiment, when it came
to their own children, the common refrain I heard was, 'I care about
social justice, but—I don't want my kid to be a guinea pig.' In other
words, things have been working out pretty well for affluent white kids,

so why rock the boat?"[8] These parents might believe in fairness and equality, but if they are to influence their own children away from contributing to racial injustice and segregation, they will need to advocate for holistic welfare of all children, including but not limited to their own. That is, they must be honest about how the smog has entered their own imaginations before they can hope to spare their own children from its destructive deceptions.

■ ■ ■

I regularly hear white adults who care about racial justice say that things will inevitably get better in the coming generations. These well-meaning people look at our increasingly racially and ethnically diverse society and assume that, with increased exposure to racial diversity, white children will naturally be more racially reconciled than their parents and grandparents. By now you will understand why we should be skeptical of these optimistic claims.

Too often we have abandoned our white children to our own silence about race. Or white parents default to vague generalities when we do speak about it, or promote a colorblind perspective that erases the very differences our children cannot help but notice. Rather than intentionally discipling our children away from racial segregation and injustice, we leave them to fend for themselves. So another generation of white Christian children bring to the church the same malformed assumptions, imaginations, and desires as have the generations before them. It's no wonder that—despite what most white Christian families, and their churches, might claim about racial reconciliation—the sins of the parents are passed on to their children.

Adding to the challenge of how to engage white children about race is a dynamic we previously examined, namely how white people think about whiteness. Being white is not equivalent to other racial or ethnic identities. That whiteness required discarding ethnicity and culture in order to access privilege means that white children face specific hurdles when grappling with their identities. This historical and sociological fact means that vague appeals to the goodness of diversity leaves white people without a way to contribute personally to racial justice.

My sons' public elementary school has made me wonder about the limits of diversity. The school, which we love, is racially and ethnically diverse. Its location on the South Side of Chicago and proximity to a major research university means that most of the students are African American with other students coming from different countries. During the fall, the school hosts International Night, and in February there is a community celebration for Black History Month. Both events are very well attended. People bring food to share, and there are student displays showcasing significant moments in history as well as information about different cultures from around the world. Our family loves attending these events, in part because our adopted sons have African-American, Latino/a, and Filipino roots. These celebrations give our family natural ways to talk about their ancestries and what it means during these early stages of life to contain so many different cultural identities. And the food is always delicious!

But what about the white children and their parents who attend these events? Obviously, those families shouldn't expect the school to organize a white history night. But without some proactive attempts to engage these children beyond celebrating someone else's cultural diversity, they will be left with the sense that their whiteness is something to be ignored or about which they should be ashamed. Discipling white children toward solidarity with the body of Christ calls for a different, more courageous approach. And it will require the entire church to participate.

■ ■ ■

To reimagine the church's ministry with children, we need to acknowledge the importance of our children in corporate worship. This is where the church's children are most consistently discipled—along with the rest of us, they are indispensable members of God's people. As the psalmist writes, "Through the praise of children and infants you have established a stronghold against your enemies, to silence the foe and the avenger" (Psalm 8:2). Children in the church are not passive recipients; they are active participants whose worship carries spiritual consequences.

Unfortunately, like much of our society, many of our churches treat children as though they are incomplete until they become adults. This belief, writes Erin Minta Maxfield-Steele, "can lead to the neglect of children's spiritual lives and to inadequate responses to their emotional and spiritual needs."[9] These needs include our children's experiences and questions about the complexities of race. When we treat our children as though they are adults-in-waiting or passive recipients of our own knowledge, we miss the chance to come alongside their lived realities such that they are oriented toward the kingdom of God. We are also forgetting how the Bible portrays children and youth. Professors Michelle Clifton-Soderstrom and David Bjorlin point out that in Scripture children "play vital roles in covenant identity and worship. In the narratives of Esther and David, for example, God ordains youth to dangerous positions, and they respond faithfully, navigating dire situations with courage and wisdom."[10] Children are to be included in worship as valued members of the church not only for their good and for the good of the entire church, but because this is how God sees them.

I want to suggest three additional reasons children should be intentionally included when the church gathers for worship, knowing that how children participate will vary due to tradition and context. First, worship *is* discipleship. This is not only true for adults. This might sound obvious, but within a society that typically separates us by age, the biblical vision of intergenerational worship and discipleship is easily forgotten.[11] When children are included in corporate worship, they become participants in the corporate formation of the entire church. As Clifton-Soderstrom and Bjorlin so beautifully put it,

Through the habit of weekly worship and the rituals that compose the liturgy, children gain a way to see the world. This is not a nihilistic world of meaninglessness and chaos, nor a utopian world where tragedy and pain are ignored, but a beautiful, broken world shot through with the glory and grandeur of God, a world God so loved that God sent Jesus, the Son of God, to bring about redemption by the power of the Holy Spirit—a world waiting to be redeemed with the help of a child.[12]

A second reason to include children in worship is how it serves as an antidote to individualism. When we look for ways to welcome children and young people to corporate worship, we are communicating that they are a part of a larger community. Theologian Marva Dawn goes as far as to claim that being "true to the Hebrew/Christian Scriptures of the Church" requires us to "reject the individualism of Western civilization."[13] This is the same hyperindividualism that hinders the attempts at racial reconciliation made by white churches.

Helping our children understand their place within the family of God means we will find ways for them to experience their place within the family. This will inevitably cause discomfort and even moments of confusion for those who have been discipled by an individualistic society. But if our children are to avoid the limiting assumptions of previous generations of white Christians, we will need to meet them in this discomfort and confusion and help them to understand the spiritual and relational riches that come from being so intimately related to their family members in Christ.

This leads to the third reason that children are necessary participants in corporate worship. Not only do our children need to be discipled away from hyper-individualism just like the rest of us, they also need tangible experiences of cross-generational community. They need the entire church for their growth into a life of robust faith. When we were children, my parents would bring my sister and me along with them to our church's midweek prayer meeting. To this day I can picture one of the older members of the congregation, a white-haired man, bent over in sincere prayer. More than almost anything I was taught, this shaped my imagination about the sincerity and tenderness of responding to God in prayer.

The experience of cross-generational community in worship provides a network of spiritual mentors as our children move through the challenges of childhood and young adulthood. Reflecting on the role played by many African-American churches in the lives of young people, La Verne Tolbert and Marilyn Brownlee write that by "inviting church members to be spiritual 'uncles' and 'aunts' to better serve children before they approach adolescence, each child is provided with extended family or role models."[14] Among many other benefits, these are precisely the sorts of relationships that hold the potential to serve as guideposts for children to what faithfulness to Christ and his church looks like *as* white people.

■ ■ ■

The spiritual formation of our white children can be reimagined as a discipleship practice away from injustice and segregation and toward solidarity, and it is imperative that we do so. Not long ago a friend of mine, a white woman who pastored a predominantly white congregation, shared a story that illustrates this urgency. A few years earlier, her suburban church had sent its young people to serve at a camp for (from the church's perspective) "kids in need from the city." When they returned, one of the youth leaders told the pastor that it had been a horrible experience. This leader reported that the urban children, all African American, were disrespectful and misbehaved. After some probing, my friend learned that the black children who were being served were the same age as the white suburban children who were serving as their counselors and leaders! Apparently, none of the white leaders, including the one who reported on the supposedly unruly black youth had seen anything wrong with this setup. Rather, their racially discipled imaginations saw the white children as leaders and the black children as those who needed to be led.

I'm afraid to consider how many similarly destructive dynamics play out each summer as white churches send their youth groups on cross-cultural missions trips around the world. For the sake of our white children, we must reimagine our ministry with them. But this ministry can also be reimagined as a practice for the entire church because the nurture of our children is the responsibility of the entire church. Without the participation of children the church is not fully itself. As we have seen, racial whiteness poses significant and unique challenges to this discipleship. However, by intentionally including children in corporate worship, we are best able to recognize those challenges and address them as opportunities for discipleship. As we turn to specific suggestions for our ministry with white children, we do so with the challenges of whiteness and the opportunities of worship to guide us.

RECOGNIZE

A white church can begin reimagining children's ministry as a discipleship practice by purposefully recognizing the impact a racialized society has on our children. Perhaps this sounds simplistic, this point having been reiterated in previous chapters. It bears emphasizing again though, given that most white parents and their churches seem to believe that by simply not being overtly racist, or by appealing to general ideas of equality ("Jesus loves the little children, all the children of the world . . .") we are doing enough to protect our children from racism.

Recognizing the impact of our society's sinful practices is not an abstract practice. For example, I know of many white churches that choose to recognize how our sexualized society impacts our children. Others realize the influence of greed and violence on the imaginations of younger Christians. Recognizing these sinful influences leads a church to specific actions in order to fashion faithful disciples. But the failure to recognize our culture's racial discipleship keeps white churches silent and inactive. Only when a white congregation begins to see the racial discipleship all of us undergo, including our children, can it begin to counteract this sinful formation as one of the challenges faced by its children.

Recognizing the power of race means a church must develop what many white people lack: a clear and precise vocabulary about race and racial injustice. Generalities are unhelpful to children who are navigating their worlds by categorizing observable differences. White adults—parents and church "uncles" and "aunts"—will need to be clear about the specific forms of prejudice and even racial superiority into which white children are culturally formed. Naming current events with words like *privilege, racism,* and *white supremacy* allows our children to recognize, confess, and move toward racial solidarity in response to the culture's deforming racial discipleship. So, for example, in response to black churches being targeted by arsonists, a white church can name the racism behind such attacks in a way that helps its youngest members see that God is concerned not simply about the generalities of this tragedy but the specific, racially motivated sins behind them.

EQUIP

My first official role in ministry was as the early childhood director at the church my wife and I were then attending. I learned a lot during those couple of years, such as how much time is required to recruit volunteers for children's ministry! Because we did not have children of our own, this role also showed me some of the challenges parents face when nurturing the faith of their sons and daughters. My supervising pastor and I sometimes discussed the tendency for busy parents to outsource the discipleship of their children to the church rather than seeing us as supporting their faithful efforts. Now that I am a busy parent myself, I better understand this tendency.

Too often, children's ministries are focused only on children; parents and other adult caregivers are an afterthought. This is a mistake, especially as we think about discipling our children toward solidarity with the body of Christ. Reimagining children's ministry includes prioritizing how parents and caregivers are equipped by the ministry to recognize that deforming discipleship and lead their children toward the kingdom of God.

The sort of preparation that a white church can provide may occasionally include specific skills that can help parents spiritually guide their white children. While these competencies are important, most of the time the church will be better situated to develop godly character in parents. That is to say, we will spend less time preparing parents for the myriad of situations they might face and instead focus on the sort of character that can respond thoughtfully and bravely to the unpredictable nature of parenting white kids in a racialized society. Dawn writes, "The first step in helping our children prevent, resist and overcome violence"—and we could add, racism—"is to recognize it in ourselves and to repent."[15]

Discipling our children away from racism and superiority begins with recognizing these sins in our own hearts. Many white parents grew up in homes where, behind closed doors, racist opinions were expressed. Others grew up with a colorblind ideology where race and racism were discussed in only the most general of terms. An equipping children's ministry will provide the space for parents to consider the impact of our racialized society on their own beliefs and assumptions. They will be invited into a community of other white parents who are coming to understand how important their personal discipleship is for their children's well-being.

A few years ago, one of the mothers in our church hosted an evening discussion with other interested moms on the topic of raising children in our racialized society. This diverse group shared their questions honestly and learned from each other ways of intentionally parenting their kids toward compassion and justice. There's no reason a group of white parents couldn't host a similar conversation in which struggles and questions related to race are shared. A group like this, facilitated perhaps by a trained church leader, would equip these parents for the uncharted parenting road ahead.

One specific way parents and caregivers need to be equipped for discipling their children has to do with how we protect them. Having pastored in an affluent white suburb and now in a black neighborhood in which some residents experience the threats of poverty, I've seen how every parent and grandparent wants to protect their children from pain. But I've also seen how middle-class culture elevates comfort and safety as some of its highest goals. It is in these affluent enclaves that Dawn's troubling observation rings truest: "Certainly one of the glaring characteristics of contemporary U.S. culture is the insistence that life be comfortable, easy, entirely without any kind of suffering."[16] This means that during difficult circumstances, our children are not prepared to consider the sources of their pain. Instead, they have been led to believe that there is nothing redemptive about pain and that the goal is to leave it behind as quickly as possible.

Almost nothing will keep white children from growing in solidarity with the racially diverse body of Christ more than our addiction to comfort. The journey against the racially unjust flow of our society is inherently painful. Learning about our nation's history of land theft, the genocide of Native Americans, the kidnapping, enslavement, rape, and torture of Africans, the exploitation of immigrant labor, and so many other terrible examples will leave a throbbing ache in our souls. If our goal is to avoid pain, we will never move beyond spiritual platitudes about racial diversity and reconciliation. And neither will our children.

Equipping white parents and caregivers means going against a culture that values protecting children from difficult feelings more than telling them the painful truth. This is where our understanding of Christian discipleship can help us move forward, despite strong cultural headwinds: following Jesus to become like Jesus in order to do what Jesus does. With Jesus as our model, our goal can never be to avoid pain. Comfort and safety must never be the highest goods for those who follow the crucified Savior whose life was marked by poverty, violence, and persecution.

When a church helps parents and caregivers embrace the painful moments of our discipleship, we are also providing the necessary framework for their children to interpret the pain that will come from pursuing racial justice and solidarity within a society that does not value true reconciliation.

EVALUATE

If corporate worship is one of the primary times children are discipled, then one simple way to reimagine our ministry with children is to evaluate our worship services. We can begin with a simple question: What does our worship service look like to our children? To this we might add, Is our worship discipling our children toward the reconciliation of the kingdom of God? With these questions in mind, let's look at a few aspects of worship that could be highlighted for the intentional discipleship of our white children.

The prayers of confession can name the sins of racism and the ways white Christians are tempted to passively accept the privilege and superiority granted to us by society. Confessing these things publicly, in prayerful language that is accessible to children, is a powerful way for even the youngest members to understand God's heart for racial reconciliation and justice. A pastor or lay leader might pray something like the following:

Lord, this week we saw examples of some of our government leaders speaking angrily about people who come from Central America. God, we know you love all people, but we also know that right now in our country people who are Latino/a are facing racism and discrimination.

Please forgive us for the prejudice in our own hearts and for the times when we could have spoken up for someone who was bullied because of their race, ethnicity, or nationality. Please help us to be courageous in how we love our neighbors, our friends, and our fellow students, no matter where they come from, what language they speak, or what color their skin is.

Sometimes the prayers will be even more specific, such as after a public display of anti-black racism in the community. The goal is to name these sensitive realities in prayer so that children are invited to move past the silence and shame that often characterize white people's engagement with race. The children, along with the rest of the church, are confronted with the power of God's grace to forgive all our sins, including our racial ones.

Another way to evaluate our worship is to ask whether white children ever see their parents or pastors submitting to people of color. As we saw in the chapter about Holy Communion, the segregated nature of white Christianity means that few of us ever have the chance to sit under the authority of a pastor or leader of color. We should not underestimate the power of the messages our children draw from this absence.

Earlier I wrote about the transracial adoption class my wife and I attended when we were preparing to adopt our first son. During the class, a white adoptive mom shared a story about an eye-opening moment when her African-American son was in kindergarten. During a routine car ride, he mustered up the courage to tell his mom that he didn't want to be black anymore. "Why not?" she asked, both surprised and concerned. "Because," he quietly replied, "black people die before they grow up." It took his mother asking her frightened son a few more questions before she understood how he came to believe something so terribly untrue. The suburb where this family lived was almost completely white. The young boy, observing his surroundings as well as the color of his own skin, drew the frightening conclusion that there were so few black people around because they die young.

In the context of our adoption class, she shared this heartbreaking story to illustrate the importance of an adoptive family's surrounding community. What similarly incorrect—and tragic—conclusions do our white children reach each Sunday when they come to worship and never observe people of color leading white people? By choosing to intentionally invite guest preachers and worship leaders of color to regularly lead the congregation, a white church sends a powerful message to its children about the breadth of the body of Christ to whom they belong.

A final way to evaluate what worship looks like to children is to ask whether or not our worship is costly. Discipleship that leads to solidarity with people of color will feel painful at times to white Christians; it will require that we relinquish unearned and destructive privileges. One of the ways to equip both adults and children for this journey is to ensure that corporate worship sometimes feels costly. Children, writes Dawn, "will not learn that discipleship demands cross-bearing if our worship practices allow them to be passive spectators or engage them in effortless monotony."[17] Is it passive monotony our children experience each Sunday, or something riskier? Are there moments that surprise our children, causing them to sit up and listen more attentively?

Over the relatively short course of our church's life there have been a few times when we were compelled to leave the building where we meet on Sundays to be present in our community. On one occasion we joined other neighborhood churches for a march down a main street to protest and pray in response to some especially horrifying instances of police brutality. Another time we walked down the block to pray near the spot where a young man had been shot and killed the night before. More than once we have sent the church out to offer to pray with our neighbors before reconvening in a public park for Holy Communion. During these outdoor services, I am always keeping an eye on the children, both for their safety as we traverse city sidewalks but also for a glimpse into what they are experiencing. By including our kids in these higher-stakes expressions of worship, we believe they are growing into a faith that expects worship to cost us something as we draw near to our neighbors.

Ministries that never make the cost of discipleship felt to its members are conforming to the consumer-oriented pattern of our society, a pattern that leaves us evaluating our worship by how we feel rather than by who we are becoming. A white church that has not evaluated the costliness of its worship is ill-prepared to disciple its members of any age toward the risky kingdom work of reconciliation.

Not every church will be ready to join a public protest, but finding equivalent ways to make unmistakably clear the congregation's commitment to the well-being of *all* God's people will go a long way toward discipling our white children. Those responsible for planning worship can ask themselves, When was the last time our children could not miss our courageous commitment to the entire body of Christ, including those Christians of color who are nearest to us?

DON'T WAIT

A final suggestion for reimagining ministry with children as a discipleship practice for the whole church is the understanding that we cannot afford to wait. When it comes to our children, parents and caregivers often err on the side of caution, not wanting to inadvertently harm them with our good intentions. But there is never a perfect moment to address racial injustice with our children. It's true that we must be thoughtful and intentional as we disciple our children away from America's racial formation. But there is no magical moment when children are suddenly ready to engage in these difficult conversations. As Harvey writes,

> It's understandable that we want to protect our kids. But if we confuse finding age-appropriate ways to tell the truth about racial harm with over insulating them, if we are too cautious because we are afraid it's just too much, if we withhold or sugarcoat the truth because we don't want to cause them suffering, we withhold the very things they need to participate in deeper and more truthful ways of living. Indeed, we withhold the very things they most need to retain their humanity.[18]

I desperately want to protect my young sons, but as cute little boys who will grow into young men of color, I know that keeping the truth from them about our racialized society will not protect them. Shielding them from the truth would make their lives exponentially more dangerous. And while it might not initially seem obvious, the same is true for white children as well. There will certainly be times when we guard our language in prayer or in a sermon because our children are present. But more often than not, we will choose not to wait, not to sugarcoat, not to shield our children from the difficult truths of the world to which God has called them as ambassadors of his reconciliation.

■ ■ ■

The nature of racial whiteness makes the healthy identity development of white children a complicated matter. A large part of coming to grips with white identity is recognizing how we have been malformed by our racialized society, how unearned racial privilege has exacted a costly price from people of color. These troubling realities alone could be enough for some to avoid the reimagined practice of ministry with children. But then, of course, we are simply abandoning our children to the deceptions of racial discipleship, leaving them to fend for themselves within a society bent on their segregation.

But because our goal is not cheap diversity but true solidarity, we can also look around our white churches with our beloved children and see enormous possibility. These young people have the God-given capacity to represent the racial justice and reconciliation of the kingdom of God, not someday but today, as valued members of the church. As they grow in their solidarity with their young siblings in Christ, the entire church will find themselves oriented more precisely toward the kingdom of God. Perhaps no other of our reimagined discipleship practices feels so fraught with danger. But neither does any other holds so much hopeful possibility.

CHAPTER EIGHT

PRACTICING PRESENCE

When we reimagine Holy Communion, gospel proclamation, the Sunday liturgy, and ministry with children, we are mostly focusing on the discipleship practices of the gathered church. But the church exists beyond its corporate worship; each week we are sent into the world as ambassadors of the reconciliation won for the universe through Jesus' death and resurrection. The fact that we are sent as individuals and families in no way diminishes the objective reality of our *koinonia*. Members of a church remain in fellowship with Christ and one another even when we are not together in person.

Because the majority of the Christian life is lived not as a gathered community but as sent people, our reimagined discipleship practices must account for following Jesus during these times. In the final chapters we will shift our attention to three discipleship practices that can shape the habits and desires of white Christians outside of the Sunday gathering. Of course, these three practices overlap with how the church worships, but they also point to how discipleship happens Monday through Saturday in the more ordinary moments of a Christian's life. The first of these practices is about how we understand and relate to place.

■ ■ ■

I am what's known in certain Christian circles as an "MK," a missionary kid. My dad was a missionary pilot who flew small airplanes into hard-to-access regions of Venezuela and Ecuador. In addition to homeschooling my sister and me when there were no English-speaking schools available, my mom closely tracked my dad's flight plan and gave him updates on rapidly changing tropical thunderstorms via the small radio that sat on the kitchen counter.

For our family, the missionary life involved many different moves— from one town to another, from one country to another, and occasionally trips back to the United States to visit family, raise money, and visit supporting churches. We were regularly on the move. After we returned to the United States for good the summer before I entered high school, we lived in the same Southern California house for four years. It was the longest my sister and I had lived in one place our entire lives.

After arriving at college in the mountains of North Carolina, I began to reflect on how strange my childhood had been. Not so much the MK thing, though that did often provoke awkward conversations with friends who held some wildly inaccurate ideas about life in South America. No, what I came to view as unique about my childhood was how often our family moved. Most of my new college friends had grown up in North Carolina or in a nearby state, and they could quickly answer the question, Where's home? I, on the other hand, dreaded the question. Each time it came up, I had to decide how much time I wanted to spend explaining my transient life. "California," I'd tell people, even though nothing about that faraway state felt like home, and I had no intentions of returning after college.

During these years, and continuing after my wife, Maggie, and I moved to the Chicago suburbs a few years later, I began to feel my sense of placelessness more keenly. I also discovered that while my childhood was unique, my rootlessness was not. In graduate school I made new friends from around the country who were preparing for Christian ministry; few of them intended to return home. Some of our suburban neighbors had grown up nearby, but many others had arrived more recently, drawn to the area for school, work in the city, or the stability and safety of suburbia.

To an extent, this transient way of life is a product of middle class, suburban, and urban life. But I noticed something interesting when we'd visit family and friends in small towns far away from the affluence of the Chicago suburbs. In many cases they had a much stronger connection to the places they lived, sometimes tracing multiple generations back in a particular town. But when it came to knowing the history and particularities of these places, they often exhibited the same benign disinterest typical among our suburban neighbors.

Over these years, as I moved from Ecuador to California to North Carolina to Chicago, I slowly realized that I wasn't as strange as I'd previously thought. My disconnectedness from any particular place was more common than my childhood had led me to believe. In fact, I've come to believe that for many Americans—especially white Americans—being rootless is normal. Most of us find nothing strange about our transience.

In this chapter I will argue that our discipleship to Jesus requires us to be rooted in a particular place. American mobility may be normal, but it is not neutral. Not only that—there's a strong link between our society's racialization and our experience of being rootless. This is not typically how we think about discipleship—or race, for that matter—so, before we get to some specific ways that place can be reimagined as a discipleship practice, we need to look at God's intention for our relationship to place. We'll also look at how race has subverted God's good intentions in order to disciple us toward segregation and injustice.

■ ■ ■

Years ago my mentor, Rev. Dr. Brenda Salter-McNeil, drew my attention to God's command to humanity in Genesis 1:28 to fill the earth and how this led to the developments of cultural and ethnic diversity in response to God's creation. This was important enough to God that in Genesis 11, when the people stopped their expansion in order to build a tower to the heavens, God confused their language so that they would scatter throughout the earth.[1]

There are two observations we need to make to understand the importance of place to our discipleship as well as how race competes with place. First, the cultural and ethnic diversity we take for granted was not incidental to God's plans for humanity. Human diversity was God's desire for his image-bearing creatures from the beginning. Second, cultural and ethnic diversity results from humanity's relationship to the creation itself. Place is what leads to the godly expressions of cultural and ethnic particularity.

Theologian Randy S. Woodley describes how this works from his vantage point as a Keetoowah Cherokee. He writes, "As a particular land . . . becomes inhabited, that group of people with a common language and common physical characteristics form a common gene pool, a common diet, a common lifestyle, et cetera. The group becomes uniquely shaped by the land as the land becomes uniquely shaped by them."[2] Woodley is describing how cultural development naturally happens. But we need to understand that this development reflects God's desire. It was God's plan for the physical creation to form his image-bearing creatures.

As social creatures, it is never only place that shapes who we are but also the other people who have been formed by a shared place. As theologian David Leong puts it, "Whatever belonging is, it involves belonging *with* and *to* others in a place. This is how communities work: people and places help us to know who we are."[3] The world God created and then called good is a world that, in its endless variety, was made to shape people and communities as culturally and ethnically unique image-bearers of the Creator. God intends his creation—that is, the places in which we are rooted—to disciple us.

We are beginning to see how the transience normal for many of us subverts God's plans for our formation. But how does this relate to our society's racialized discipleship that we are aiming to counteract? To see this connection we need to step back in history.

■ ■ ■

The story of how race became more powerful than place for the formation of people and communities is long and intricate. And though our focus has been on race in America, this story reveals the global nature of racial injustice and oppression. Theologians and historians have documented it in compelling detail. For our purposes, we will sketch this history in three movements: Jesus' particularity, European colonialism, and racial hierarchy in the United States.

Central to Paul's understanding of what Jesus accomplished on the cross is the mystery of Gentile inclusion in the Jewish people of God. We who had previously been foreigners and aliens to God's promise have been brought near through Israel's Messiah, grafted as wild branches into "the nourishing sap from the olive root" (Romans 11:17). In Professor Willie James Jennings's words, "We Gentiles were outsiders to Israel. We were at the margins. So our engagement with Jesus was engagement from the margins, not from the center of power or privilege."[4]

But this status as welcomed outsiders would be challenged and ultimately erased when the seat of Christian power shifted to Europe. A heresy began to develop, what theologians call supersessionism, in which "the church replaces Israel in the mind and heart of God."[5] In this theological move, Jesus' Jewishness was downplayed, along with the central role of Israel as God's elected people who were to bless the world through the Messiah. "Here was a process of discerning Christian identity that, because it had jettisoned Israel from its calculus of the formation of Christian life, created a conceptual vacuum that was filled by the European."[6]

No longer did the European church, with its growing wealth and influence, understand itself as welcomed outsiders. Now, in place of Jesus' particularities—culture, ethnicity, history, religion, and so on—through which God had acted, European identity was placed at the center of the Christian experience. This proved an especially destructive development when combined with the next historical movement we'll consider: colonialism.

As the European nations began their colonial expansion projects, they did so under the influence of this malformed Christianity. Christian explorers, settlers, and conquerors came with imaginations which had been formed to see themselves not only as standard-bearers for the faith, but also as those with the power to define the places and people they encountered. Rather than coming from the margins—outsiders grafted into the people of God—the colonizers imagined themselves at the center. And rather than looking to the creation itself and the peoples it had formed in these "new" lands, the European explorers themselves became the norm by which everyone and everything were understood. Jennings observes that the "significance of this transformation cannot be overstated. The earth itself was barred from being a constant signifier of identity. Europeans defined Africans and all others apart from the earth even as they separated them from their lands."[7]

The explorers were aided in their efforts to claim lands and conquer their inhabitants by a series of papal bulls. The Doctrine of Discovery allowed European nations to claim these places as their own and to treat the people they found there as they saw fit. One such papal bull, *Dum Diversas*, issued in 1452, allowed the King of Portugal and his representatives to "to invade, search out, capture, vanquish, and subdue all . . . pagans whatsoever, and other enemies of Christ wheresoever placed . . . and to reduce their persons to perpetual slavery."[8]

Into this toxic mix of warped theology, colonial expansion, and cultural superiority stepped thinkers and theologians who, upon encountering people and cultures new to them, began categorizing them in relation to their own standards of cultural supremacy. One such man, a Spanish Jesuit named José de Acosta Porres, came to Peru and developed a barbarian typology of the people he met. Not only did he determine what sort of governments would be best suited for each class of "barbarian," he also described which form of conversion would be necessary for each. He believed some could be reasoned with; others would need their existing rituals to be appropriated by the church; while still others would need to be converted by force.[9]

Now we can see the final movement of how the human construction of race subverted the power God intended for place. With colonialism spreading into regions previously unknown to European power and its Christianity, what we know today as race began to develop in earnest. A disembodied Christianity which no longer looked to God's creation for understanding had to find another way to interpret and form the world. As Woodley writes, "Euro-western, hierarchical worldviews set humanity up, over and above the rest of creation. In such a view it makes no sense to become intimate with creation."[10] And so, in place of the creation, a system of racial categorization evolved in the European imagination. In these new lands, racial whiteness replaced ethnic distinction and became the lens through which the world was viewed, understood, and categorized. Not only did the European colonialists and settlers evaluate lands and their inhabitants through a racialized lens, that same racial power detached them from the new land and its God-intended role to shape people. Race, not place, claimed ultimate formational power.

The system of race that developed was not one of simple cultural difference but one that from the beginning privileged whiteness. The narrative of racial difference was advanced through the gaze of whiteness, an imagination that developed in direct response to powerful Christian nations' detachment from place. A story that began when Europeans erased Jesus' particularities in order to place themselves at the center of Christian power continued at the founding of a new nation whose founders understood themselves in distinctly Christian terms and who saw nothing wrong with displacing and killing the land's inhabitants, kidnapping and enslaving Africans, and discarding their own ethnic and cultural particularities in order to seize the promises and power of racial whiteness. This is what results when God's desires for the creation are forsaken for a racial discipleship of our own making.

■ ■ ■

At this point we might think that by simply re-prioritizing place we can resist our society's racialized discipleship. However, because of the legacy of systemic racism, the places we inhabit have been severely marred by the narrative of racial difference. The places we live, no matter how transiently we may be there, reveal "how cultural patterns become physical structures, and how impersonal systems grow to protect the interests of those in power over time."[11] Our towns, suburbs, and neighborhoods have all been fundamentally altered by a racial gaze which has organized and displaced people according to the twisted logic of race.

It doesn't take long to identify the arrangements of racial segregation in our cities and suburbs today. There are no current legal reasons for these patterns. Ostensibly anyone can live anywhere they like, as long as they can afford to. Yet this history of housing in America is one that was shaped by *de jure* segregation; federal law and real estate policies determined where people could live based on race. While those laws have since been repealed, we discover how little has changed when we compare contemporary demographic maps of a city to older maps showing legal segregation,.[12]

In other words, it's not enough to claim that we care about the places in which we find ourselves. For place to regain its God-intended formational power, we must also understand the histories of these places and how they have been altered by the power of race. We will need to ask about the people who lived here before us. Why do some people live in this area of town while others live over there? Why are all of the low-rent apartments concentrated in that area of the otherwise affluent suburb? Why do children in that area of the city have access to high-quality public schools while the families in this part of the city have to make do with overcrowded classrooms and dilapidated buildings?

■ ■ ■

Before considering how our intentional presence in a particular place can disciple white Christians toward solidarity with the body of Christ, we should acknowledge how unfamiliar this conversation is to most of us. Discipleship cannot happen in detachment from place, yet this is exactly how much of white Christianity operates. Because we have come to see ourselves as disembodied from the creation, how we imagine our involvement with a place and its history is rather shallow. Though we might talk about reaching our neighbors with the gospel, we rarely consider how they—or we—must be understood in relationship to the places we live in.

I think about this deficiency in our discipleship when I visit other churches. There is rarely anything in our church buildings that would indicate *where* a church is located. Often times our sanctuaries have the feel of a franchise; nothing in them would describe to an out-of-town guest what is distinct about the place and its people.

A number of years ago, Maggie and I spent a few days in Napa Valley. When we made the requisite visits to a couple of the local wineries, we learned about the concept of terroir, the many environmental variables that influence a wine's characteristics. When making wines, expert winemakers consider the soil, weather, and other factors that will affect the final taste of any particular vintage. A wine's terroir tells the person drinking it some important things about where it comes from, and that *that* wine could *only* come from that particular place.

In a racialized society, it's rare to experience terroir in a white church. Because we have been detached in any meaningful sense from place, our discipleship takes on an abstract quality. We may not do this purposefully, but this tendency betrays how completely our imaginations have been discipled by race. But by reimagining intentional presence to our particular places, our churches will begin to experience the latent potential of God's creation to disciple us toward the kingdom of God.

■ ■ ■

Compared with the discipleship practices we've already explored, the practice of presence is one many white ministries will not have previously considered. This does not mean that a lot of new activity will be required, but it will likely involve a different sort of commitment. For people who have been discipled by our society to imagine themselves removed from creation, able to move here and there with little thought about the consequences, the decision to prioritize rootedness and presence will not come easily.

PARTICULARITY

To begin with, white Christians need to return to the source of our severance from creation and encounter the profound significance of Jesus' particularity. If the origins of race can be partly traced to the separation of Jesus from his Jewish identity, then we must reacquaint ourselves with this essential theme of salvation history. Jesus' Jewishness was not an accident of history. This matters for two reasons.

First, by elevating Jesus' Jewish particularity we are highlighting the important thread from the Old Testament through the New in which Israel's election to be a blessing for the world is fulfilled in Jesus. The Gentile inclusion in God's covenant is accomplished precisely because God kept his promises to Israel. We who are Gentiles are the joyful recipients of God's generosity through Israel and Israel's Messiah. We are welcomed outsiders. In contrast, America's racial discipleship tells white people that we are at the center, that our experience is the one by which all others are evaluated and judged.

Many of the Asian American members of our church can tell stories of white people who want to know where they're from. When they reply that they're from Chicago, the response is often, "No, I mean, where are you *really* from?" In the eyes of the white questioner, the Asian American is a permanent foreigner, no matter how many previous generations have made America home. As a white person I will never be asked this question. Here's another example: many of the African American women I know have been approached by white women who, after complementing them on their hair, ask if they can touch it. Even worse, some of these friends have had white people touch their hair without even asking! Because we have been formed to understand ourselves as the cultural center, the normative gaze through which others are viewed and interpreted, white people often find nothing objectionable about taking such thoughtless license. I expect, though, that if the experience were reversed, those of us who are white would be horrified at having our bodies treated as a curiosity to be commented about and touched without our permission.

In both of these disturbing examples, white people are looking at a person of color and interpreting their embodied presence through the lens of race. They are engaging these particular image-bearers of God through the warped—and dehumanizing—white gaze. By discipling white Christians into the true story of our inclusion as outsiders into the people of God, we decenter our experience. We discover that our perspective and assumptions are not neutral; neither are they the standard through which others should be viewed.

A second reason it's important to elevate Jesus' Jewish particularity is to expose white Christians to the implications of the incarnation to our own lives. Of course the incarnation—God taking on flesh—is universally important for how Jesus takes onto himself the consequences of sin. But the incarnation also speaks to the sacredness of our own particularities. That Jesus was born among a particular people means all people are valuable, and we are valuable not despite our distinctions but within them.

For white people, this means we must come to see people of color beyond the blinders of race. This does not mean being colorblind. Rather, we must see our neighbors as they see themselves. So we don't see our Asian-American neighbor as a perpetual foreigner. Neither do we exoticize our African-American coworker, reaching to touch her hair in complete disregard for her feelings. It also means that we think about ourselves more carefully. Most white people do not grow up thinking of ourselves as part of a shared identity. Yet, as we've seen, we have been shaped by racial whiteness, and it does no good to believe otherwise.

As white Christians develop a lived theology of Jesus' Jewish particularity, we will move from the center to the margins, no longer assuming our experience and norms as the natural standard by which everyone else is measured. We'll also find the theological imagination to more accurately relate with and love our neighbors of color, even while more correctly understanding ourselves.

ROOTS

Another way to reimagine the practice of presence is to ask white Christians to make a long-term commitment to place. Such is the extent to which we have been formed by racial discipleship that such an invitation will strike most white Christians as strange and constricting. While it's never fun to say goodbye, most of us believe that it is normal for our friends and family members to move away for the promise of a more lucrative salary, a more comfortable climate, a prestigious graduate school, or a better cost of living. We have become a society of wanderers. But there is nothing inevitable about this, and once we understand God's purposes for his creation, we can reevaluate the questionable virtues of transience.

Author Jonathan Wilson-Hartgrove defines this sort of commitment to place as the wisdom of stability. "To practice stability," he writes, "is to learn to love both a place and its people."[13] I have heard more than one pastor of younger urban congregations exhort their members to commit to their neighborhoods. "If you had planned on staying here one year," they might say, "commit to staying two. If you planned on staying here three years, plan to stay five." These pastors know that many in their congregations came to the city for school, a job, or a temporary urban experience. They also know that if their members are to be truly impacted by their time in the city, they need to stop thinking of themselves as detached consumers of what the city has to offer and begin understanding their lives as being intertwined with their neighbors.

What might an intentional commitment to place look like? For starters, it will involve a curiosity about local history. Rather than doing detached or disembodied ministry, a white church will begin to learn about what transpired before their arrival. For a younger church this will mean learning about the histories of other churches in the areas. For long-established churches this will involve dusting off the archives and learning how the Spirit has been active among the congregation in particular ways. This curiosity will lead to ministry priorities and initiatives that align with what God has already been doing in that place.

One of my friends, Chris Harris, pastors a Church of God in Christ congregation in our neighborhood. Because his church has outgrown its facility, my friend moved the church to another one a mile away. Though they will only be in this location for a few years while building a new sanctuary, he has made sure to learn about the history of their new building. It happens that this church sanctuary was the location in 1955 for the funeral of Emmet Till, the black teenager who was kidnapped, mutilated, and shot to death by two white men while visiting relatives in Mississippi. Emmett's mother, Mamie Till Mobley, chose to open her son's casket at his funeral, thus showing the nation the horrors of white mob law in Jim Crow America.

Because Pastor Harris understands this history, his congregation chose to engage the community's youth with programming that discusses the history of racism in our nation and how it impacts young black women and men today. He is purposefully leading his church to speak directly to the lived experiences, challenges, and opportunities of his community. Having worshiped in his church, I know that barely a Sunday goes by when the church is not reminded of the specific place to which they have been called. Most of our churches will not have such vivid moments to respond to, but every church can discover something about the history of their place to which they can relate intentionally and fruitfully.

White churches can also attach putting down roots with the process of becoming a church member. When people are invited to join a church, they are asked to make certain promises about how they will live and what they will commit to as members. Rarely, though, do these promises have anything to do with that congregation's location. In fact, in many denominations it is common to simply transfer one's membership from one local church to another, with no thought about how place might impact how membership promises are embodied.

About half of our congregation's members did not grow up in or near our community. They have moved to Chicago for school or work, or they come to our church from a different area of the city. This means that at least half our people do not have personal experience with our community aside from worship on Sundays and the occasional service opportunity. Because so much of our ministry is contextualized to the uniqueness of our neighborhood, it's important that people learn about its history and the current dynamics that shape it.

We've attempted this in a variety of ways, including a tour of the neighborhood led by a long-term resident, a yearly community workshop that explores race in our local context, and a requirement that each member of our leadership team participate in a weekend trip through civil rights sites in the American South in order to understand some of the historical forces that gave birth to our neighborhood. But what we do most consistently is include a discussion about our community's history in our membership classes. We make sure that new members have a basic understanding of some important historical events, including the role played by African American churches in supporting our neighbors throughout previous generations. Perhaps more importantly, we are able to communicate that engaging with this history is part of what it means to be a member of the church. We want potential members to understand that what we do as a church is framed by who our neighbors are and by what God has done among them long before our arrival.

A final way to help white Christians commit to place is to remind them that it will often be difficult. Wilson-Hartgrove writes about the desert fathers, who warned their younger members about "the 'noonday devil' who attacks *after* one commits to stay and begins to feel the heat of high noon."[14] Like any commitment, deciding to reject the American temptation of constant mobility will bring about a host of challenges. There is nothing especially charming about staying put. Rather than moving to greener pastures, we choose to pay attention to the parched areas in our own lives and those within our community. Rather than chasing a higher salary or more prestigious career, we remain out of the limelight, faithfully attending to the small things in our neighborhoods and on our blocks.

It is important that when we invite people to commit to their place, we also prepare them to put down roots. After all, staying is hard. Community is messy. Getting involved in the local school council or block club is anything but glamorous. Getting to know our neighbors means making ourselves vulnerable to their suffering. These inevitable dynamics have often pushed white Christians to move, to look longingly at the glittering promises of a new location, whether that be the comfort of the suburb, the allure of the city, or the peace of a small town.

We can most effectively prepare people for these difficult moments when we remind one another that Jesus calls us to be faithful; fruitfulness is the Holy Spirit's responsibility. As we discern our commitment through the metrics of faithfulness, we will begin to see the spiritual fruit we would have otherwise missed. After all, the kingdom of God often looks like mustard seeds and yeast, evidence of God's presence with us that can only be seen by those who are present to their place.

MUTUALITY

The practice of presence is also experienced through mutuality with our neighbors. As white Christians begin to see ourselves as welcomed outsiders and our own experience not as the neutral lens through which neighbors of color are viewed, we are open to new possibilities of interconnectedness nurtured by the place we share.

Racial discipleship works to convince us of our independence from both place and other people. On the other hand, when reattached to creation, discipleship to Jesus leads us to see how interdependent we are with all of our neighbors. Our very bodies, theologian Brian Bantum claims, "material as they are, are never disconnected from others."[15]

While mutuality is something we should teach, I've come to believe that white Christians most need to see it visibly expressed by their leaders. Because we have been discipled to see ourselves as detached from place and in many ways from our neighbors, we mostly engage with people of color from a posture of power. Cross-cultural missions trips and local service projects are usually done in the role of provider. Rarely do we see examples of white churches engaging with people of color from a position of mutuality, much less from a position of need. So, while we might articulate a theology of mutuality, the practice of presence requires that we see it lived out.

As far as I know, I am the only white pastor in our neighborhood, and ours is the only nonblack church. Over the years there have been many, many times when I have needed the material assistance and wisdom of African-American colleagues. They have supported us financially, lent us their facilities, opened their networks to us, counseled me through complicated situations, and publicly applied their credibility to our fledgling ministry. In many of these moments our church has had a front row seat to my need; they have seen how our church has been tangibly helped by our ministry partners in the neighborhood.

I'd like to claim that this strategy was provoked by my own humility and wisdom, but the truth is that I mostly experience mutuality through my own desperation. I genuinely need my colleagues of color. White ministry leaders will need to put themselves in situations where mutuality is their only option. Choosing to step into unknown ministry opportunities, to accept invitations to collaborate with a ministry of color, or to simply ask God for the chance to experience the interconnectedness of the kingdom of God will all lead to those moments of godly desperation when mutuality is our only option.

SABBATH

My final suggestion for growing into the practice of presence to place is to prioritize the weekly day of worship and rest. While most churches would never discount the other nine commandments, for some reason we are quick to overlook the one about Sabbath. Yet a weekly day of rest and worship can help us honor the places to which God has called us.

The biblical invitation to sabbath is almost always related to the land. It is not only people who need a day to cease our work, the land itself is meant to rest. In Leviticus 25, God commanded his people to give their land a sabbath rest every seven years. His promise to them was that, even as they ceased their agricultural work, God would provide for each of their needs.

Not only does a weekly sabbath offer the gift of nonproductivity, it also reminds us of our connection to God's creation. This reminder is especially important for those of us who live distant from the agricultural seasons that gave rhythm to the lives of our spiritual ancestors. I realize this might sound rather abstract, but it is my experience that when a church begins to claim the extravagant gift of a weekly day of rest, its members also begin to notice their dependence on the land.

Woodley writes that all "land is holy because God is holy. It is sacred because the land, and all creation, is considered to be a gift from God."[16] The sabbath gift of time can lead us to see what so many white Christians have long missed, that the land too is a gift from God, a holy gift by which God will form a holy people. Living into the weekly rhythm of sabbath rest can lead us to a keenly felt attachment to our place, which is a necessary part of leaching some of the malicious power of race.

■ ■ ■

I close with three caveats. First, the practice of presence to place does not preclude the possibility of moving. Scripture makes it clear that Christians are sometimes called elsewhere as ambassadors of reconciliation. The difference is between being sent and leaving. Rather than leaving to chase the American Dream, Christians discern God's call in community and then are blessed and sent in obedience to it.

Second, while I have highlighted the transience of many white Christians, many of our neighbors do not experience the privilege of mobility. The strictures of racial segregation and poverty keep many people stuck in environments that wreak havoc on their families and communities. Or, through neighborhood redevelopment or gentrification, they are forced to leave behind beloved neighborhoods and communities. The practice of presence to place should never be used to romanticize someone else's marginalization. Rather, when white Christians who have the privilege of mobility practice presence, they will be led to embodied solidarity with those neighbors to whom that privilege has never been extended.

Finally, it's worth reiterating how very countercultural this practice is. Calling people to remain when the temptation to leave is so attractively presented by our culture is bound to be met with confusion and at least initially with resistance. But over time, as white Christians discover their place as welcomed outsiders among God's people, the invitation to remaining present to a place and its people will be heard as a compelling invitation to experience the embodied hospitality of God and his people.

CHAPTER NINE

PRACTICING SALVATION
FROM SUPERIORITY

I LOVE THE STORY OF THE EARLY CHURCH'S exciting first days found in the book of Acts. There are so many great moments as the good news about Jesus rapidly spreads through regions and cultures, calling together the most surprising collections of women and men. Of all these stories, my favorite might be about the time the Christians caused a riot. There was often trouble when Paul and his companions arrived in a new city and began testifying to what God had accomplished through Jesus' death and resurrection. In fact, by the time we get to Acts 24:5, Paul has a reputation for stirring up trouble "all over the world." But even with trouble seeming to follow them everywhere they went, the riot in Ephesus was astonishing.

The trouble began when Paul baptized a small group of new believers into the power of the Holy Spirit and then began speaking in the synagogue, "arguing persuasively about the kingdom of God" (Acts 19:8). For two years Paul proclaimed Jesus with power. Within this culturally diverse city both Jews and Greeks accepted the gospel and became disciples of Jesus. In doing so, they turned away from the idols and ideologies that had previously governed their lives. The problem was that Ephesus was home to a major temple to the Greek goddess Artemis. In addition to providing much of the religious climate for the city, the temple was also a major economic driver. Acts 19:24 tells us that the demand for shrines to Artemis "brought in a lot of business for the craftsmen there." Because many of the Ephesians had accepted the good news about the kingdom of God, they no longer supported the temple economy, and some of Ephesus's leading citizens got nervous enough to provoke the entire city into an uproar.

I am fascinated by this story because in all my life as a Christian I have yet to see evangelism instigate a riot in the United States. I am grateful to have been raised in traditions of Christianity that believed the gospel of Jesus was so good that it has to be shared with the world. The missionaries my parents served in Venezuela and Ecuador believed so completely in this gospel that they left behind comforts, learned new languages, and sent their children to boarding schools for the opportunity to share this good news. Yet when it comes to disrupting the status quo of our racialized society—a society, like that in Ephesus, which is often at odds with the kingdom of God—I've never seen white Christianity's gospel come anywhere close to provoking the kinds of disturbance we see in Acts.

A few years ago while attending a ministry conference, I listened as one of America's most well-known pastors described the major transitions he had experienced over the course of his ministry. He described these transitions as second conversions. After converting to Jesus as a young person, he went on to have a variety of "aha!" moments in which his ministry took on additional characteristics of the kingdom of God. One of these was his theological discovery that women, like men, have been gifted for every kind of leadership within the church. Another of these second conversions had to do with the racial segregation that is normal within white Christianity. Through his relationships with a few African American pastors, this white leader realized that the segregation he had previously assumed to be neutral actually contradicted the gospel he passionately proclaimed each Sunday.

I think this pastor's story is illustrative. For many white Christians, our conversion to justice is secondary, occurring sometime after our first conversion to Jesus. And secondary conversions, no matter how important, will never be as important as the first. They are, in a word, optional.

. . .

As we continue thinking about discipleship practices for the sent church, it is important to consider how the ways we share the gospel can orient us toward the kingdom of God. The assumption that the church makes new disciples is central to our identity as Christ's ambassadors and evidence of our obedience to his commandments. But does this mean that we should be stirring up riots with our evangelism? Maybe the fact that so many Americans consider themselves to be Christians or are at least familiar with Christianity explains why the gospel generally does not stir up much visible opposition. By now, though, we have seen some of the many ways that our racialized society is actually hostile to the reconciled kingdom of God that Jesus proclaimed and brought near. Should we not expect at least some amount of resistance and disturbance when, like the early church, we testify persuasively to the kingdom of God?

I see at least three reasons why the gospel, as many white Christians understand and proclaim it, causes so few disturbances within our racialized society. The first has to do with the dualistic spirituality that separates people's souls from their bodies. In this view, the priority of evangelism is to save souls for an eternity with God; everything else is secondary. An evangelistic sermon climaxes with a call to conversion without ever meaningfully addressing the material realities in the new Christian's life. So this new believer is left to assume that the point of the Christian life is salvation from sin for heaven.

A second reason for our culturally palatable evangelism is the hyper-individualism we've discussed in previous chapters. Because white Christianity tends to view people as self-contained individuals, we can miss significant relational connections and networks. We are blind, for example, to the cultural privilege into which white people are born in this country. Similarly, the generational oppression and disempowerment attached to the African-American experience is generally invisible to people who believe so strongly in people's ability to determine their own future. From this individualistic vantage point, inviting people to follow Jesus will almost never disrupt the societal forces that resist the kingdom of God in their lives.

Finally, in the previous chapter we observed how race detaches people from place. When Paul began proclaiming the gospel in Ephesus, both the Jews and the Greeks immediately saw how the kingdom of God challenged the deep cultural and religious assumptions of their city. But our detachment from place blinds us to how we have been impacted by our society as well as to how the gospel may very well be an offense to that same society.

Taken together, these three tendencies of white Christianity contribute to making our evangelism tolerable to society. While individual people may disagree with our beliefs, a culture infected with the narrative of racial difference and white superiority does not feel threatened by our discipleship.

■ ■ ■

There is, though, another reason some white Christians don't experience the Ephesus-like tumult when we share the gospel, and that's because we don't share the gospel. In general terms, white Christians who are committed to evangelism have often been disinterested in racial justice, while those white Christians who are committed to it often seem squeamish about sharing their faith with others. For much of white Christianity it seems impossible to hold together evangelism and racial justice. It has often seemed that we must pick one or the other.

I've come to understand this unholy bifurcation to be one of white Christianity's defining attributes. As we will see, other expressions of American Christianity have not had any problem evangelistically proclaiming the gospel and pursuing justice.

In the summer of 2014, an African-American man named Eric Garner died on the streets of Staten Island after being put in a chokehold by police officers. His last gasping words, "I can't breathe," became a rallying cry for grieving and angry protestors around the country. Later that fall, a ministry colleague from the neighborhood called me. He was asking churches on the South Side of Chicago to take to the streets after our worship services that coming Sunday. He explained that our neighbors needed to see that the churches stood in solidarity with those who felt threatened and unsafe even as we embodied God's peace with our visible presence.

Most of our church's members bundled up after the worship service on that chilly Sunday and walked into the street. Some held signs asking for justice; parents held their children's hands, and some pushed strollers along the sidewalks. At one of the main streets, our small march merged with three other churches, and now we filled the street, curb to curb, as we walked south. We sang and shouted and prayed before laying our bodies down in an intersection, an expression of solidarity with the Garner family and the many in our city who have lost family members and friends to gun violence.

I learned a lot that cold Sunday morning, but what regularly comes to mind about that day is just how normal it was for so many of the African American Christians who made up our marching congregation. For most of these Christians there was nothing disjointed about gathering to worship—lifting voices in praise, sitting under the preached Word, giving tithes and offerings, calling nonbelievers to give their lives to Jesus—and then being sent into the streets to cry out for racial justice.

How different from most expressions of white Christianity! When it comes to evangelism, captive as we are to a dualistic, individualistic, and disembodied perspective, we leave white Christians to view racial justice as an optional add-on to our faith. We leave it for a potential second conversion somewhere down the line.

The consequences of not connecting racial justice with the gospel are significant. For one, this simplistic form of evangelism leaves white Christians blinded to our privilege. Many new disciples accept God's grace extended through Jesus because of an awareness of our own sinful desperation, but the nature of racial privilege means that very few white people will ever experience it as something we need saving from. America's racial discipleship keeps white people from seeing how our imaginations and assumptions have been discipled toward racial superiority. So we respond to the amazing news that God has made a way for sinners like us to be saved without ever realizing our complicity with racial privilege and injustice. We enter Christianity with our privilege unquestioned and the devious narrative of racial difference and superiority still freely shaping our imaginations.

Not only is our own discipleship stunted by this bifurcated gospel, so are our relationships with Christians of color. Instead of being shown how the kingdom of God stands opposed to a society that inculcates racism and segregation, new white Christians are left to tacitly assume the compatibility of the two. For Christians of color who cannot help but see through this lie, the possibility of trustworthy solidarity with white Christians is prevented from the very beginning.

■ ■ ■

One Sunday in the fall of 1898, thirty-three years after the end of the Civil War, the Reverend Francis Grimké stood before his church in Washington, DC, and preached a sermon titled "The Negro Will Never Acquiesce as Long as He Lives." After a period of federal intervention in the South, Jim Crow violence had returned with a vengeance, and Grimké, like so many other black Christians, looked on in horror as a white, supposedly Christian, nation violently oppressed its African-American citizens. After describing the discouragement and horrors faced by black people, the pastor turned his attention to white churches, saying, "Another discouraging circumstance is to be found in the fact that the pulpits of the land are silent on these great wrongs. The ministers fear to offend those to whom they minister." He then noted the sorts of sins that white Christians were comfortable calling out—alcohol, gambling, breaking the sabbath—before wondering at their silence in response to so much visible racial terror. I can almost hear the anger and confusion in his voice as he revealed the hypocrisy of the white churches and their pastors. "They are eloquent in their appeals to wipe out these great wrongs, but when it comes to Southern brutality, to the killing of Negroes and despoiling them of their civil and political rights, they are, to borrow an expression from Isaiah, 'dumb dogs that cannot bark.'" [1]

In this lament, Rev. Grimké joined contemporaries like Frederick Douglass and Ida B. Wells in looking to white Christianity for support, only to find indifference and antagonism. Years later, the Reverend Dr.

Martin Luther King Jr. would sit in a small Alabama jail cell and write his epistle to the white churches who had quietly sat out the civil rights movement. He recalled his time organizing in the South for the most basic rights, all while facing sustained opposition from powerful government officials. In the midst of this great struggle, he wrote, "I have heard many ministers say: 'Those are social issues, with which the gospel has no real concern.' And I have watched many churches commit themselves to a completely other worldly religion which makes a strange, un-Biblical distinction between body and soul, between the sacred and the secular."[2] Despite his years of having been let down by white Christians, he still couldn't help but marvel at their disinterest in the plight of their fellow Christians.

By not following the example of many black churches and other churches of color and holding together gospel proclamation with racial justice, white Christians have consistently sidelined ourselves in the battles waged against our family in Christ. Worse yet, we have contributed to their oppression.

Discipling white Christians away from racial segregation and injustice and toward solidarity must begin at the beginning, with how we invite white people to follow Jesus as his disciples. We cannot afford to leave new white Christians blinded to their privilege and ignorant of their deformed racial imaginations. We cannot settle for hoped-for second conversions to racial justice. For too many Christians these other conversions never come and others, after their eyes are opened to racial injustice, come to doubt a faith that was not honest with them about their sinful complicity with racial injustice.

Reimagining evangelism as a discipleship practice allows white Christians to choose solidarity with the body of Christ at the very beginning of our discipleship to Jesus. Instead of supporting a divided Christianity that separates the gospel from justice, this practice invites people to give their lives to following Jesus into the kingdom of God, a kingdom which we proclaim with joy and demonstrate with justice.

■ ■ ■

To reimagine evangelism in a manner congruent with the experience of many churches of color, we need to highlight two familiar words:

discipleship and *kingdom*. Though discipleship frames this entire book, when it comes to evangelism we often set it aside, imagining the practicalities of following Jesus as coming sometime after conversion.

Many churches focus on conversion—discipleship, we seem to assume, is something that happens on its own. But this is backward. Instead, as Dallas Willard writes, we should "intend to make disciples and let converts 'happen.'"[3] The distinction is important if evangelism is to be reimagined as a discipleship practice leading to solidarity. By inviting white people who don't yet know Jesus to give their entire lives to following him, we are, right from the beginning, setting the trajectory for whole-life reorientation around the person and priorities of Jesus.

Beginning with discipleship also reckons with the dualism, individualism, and disembodiment that weakens the power of the gospel to confront the injustices of our society. While the call to follow Jesus includes salvation and assurance of eternal life, it does not end with that. Rather, the entire person, within the particular physical landscape that has shaped her, is called to join the people of God as ambassadors of Christ's reconciliation.

The call to discipleship, then, is a call in which persons, communities, and places matter. Whereas many forms of evangelism leave white Christians blind to our racial sins and detached from the body of Christ, the invitation to become a disciple of Jesus carries far more potential. By recognizing the significance of our bodies, the community to which we belong, and the places that have formed us and to which we are called, discipleship can immediately begin opening the eyes of white Christians to our racial privilege and warped assumptions about racial difference and supremacy.

Beginning with whole-life discipleship rather than disembodied conversion also prepares white Christians for the costly nature of following Jesus. We saw how important this is when it comes to the spiritual formation of white children, but it's no less critical for adults. It's true that following Jesus through the indwelling of the Holy Spirit provides us with innumerable spiritual gifts. Even in the most desperate of circumstances, disciples of Jesus over the generations have testified that life is far better with Jesus than without him. Even so, Jesus promised his disciples that following him involves carrying our crosses. Persecution, opposition, abandonment, and betrayal are all marks of discipleship to our crucified Savior.

Evangelistic invitations given to white people will be heard through the static of our society's racial discipleship, which aims our desires toward privilege, comfort, and security. If we expect white Christians to be oriented away from these segregating desires, it is essential that they understand from the beginning that the invitation to Jesus is dangerous. It will require sacrifice and moments when dying to sin feels like a death. As white Christians discover how our racial identities have deformed us and wounded our neighbors of color, the invitation to discipleship will have prepared us to remain present to the work of God in spite of the pain of these moments.

How do we invite people not simply to conversion but to follow Jesus with their whole lives as his disciples? This is where we must highlight the kingdom. Willard writes that we "lead people to become disciples of Jesus by *ravishing them* with a vision of life in the kingdom of the heavens in the fellowship of Jesus. And you do this by proclaiming, manifesting, and teaching the kingdom to them in the manner learned from Jesus himself."[4]

With our attention in these pages focused on the ravages of racial injustice, it is possible that we forget just how *good* the kingdom of God is. But the reality of the kingdom among us is the beautiful reality by which God intends to recreate our deepest desires and loves. It *is* a ravishing vision! And, as author James Choung points out, Jesus has made this kingdom available to us now.

> We are invited into a space where God is really in charge, where what he wants to happen actually does happen. It's a place of love, joy, peace, patience, kindness, goodness, gentleness, faithfulness, and self-control. It's about service and love, not dominations and oppression. It's inclusive instead of exclusive, a place for all where our relationships are right, good, and healthy.[5]

Whereas much of the evangelism within white Christianity relies on a promise of what Jesus will do for the individual, the invitation to follow Jesus into his kingdom introduces the hopeful promise of what God is doing for the entire universe through Jesus' reign. Though the invitation will inevitably bring hardships, none of these lessens the essential goodness of the kingdom.

And whereas many evangelistic invitations leave white Christians content in our segregation, the call to follow Jesus into his kingdom makes explicit the reconciled community to which all Christians belong. We are not isolated believers with Jesus hidden in our hearts. Rather, we have joined a diverse multitude who have been called to represent Christ's reign of righteousness, on earth as it is in heaven. Thus, in a manner representative of the ethnically and culturally diverse early church, white Christians must be discipled *from the beginning* to see themselves as belonging to those from whom our society's racial discipleship has long segregated us.

■ ■ ■

With our attention precisely focused on discipleship and the kingdom of God, we can reimagine evangelism as a discipleship practice for solidarity. Rather than abandoning new Christians to privilege and supremacy, white churches can invite people to follow Jesus into the kingdom of God, to become like Jesus in order to do what Jesus does. Here is a foundation strong enough to confess the sins of segregation and racial injustice while building toward solidarity with the body of Christ.

TOGETHER

The first way of reimagining evangelism is to realize that bearing witness to Jesus is something a church or ministry does together. The nature of white Christianity is such that we mostly imagine sharing the gospel as a solitary responsibility: one person invites another person to place their faith in Jesus. But in order for evangelism to function as a discipleship practice, we must remember what would have been commonly understood by the early church, that making disciples is something the church does together.

Think again about that troublemaking church in Ephesus. The dominant society was nervous about the new Christians not because a few of them engaged in one-on-one evangelism but because of their collective witness to the kingdom of God and its one Lord Jesus. I don't mean to downplay the importance of individual Christians sharing our faith. The Holy Spirit equips some with the gift of evangelism and, given Paul's instructions to Timothy, it's a safe assumption that all ministry leaders are expected to intentionally share the gospel (2 Timothy 4:5). But by highlighting discipleship into the kingdom, a church can show how evangelism is something that every member contributes to.

In the area of racial justice and reconciliation, this togetherness is accented by how a white church responds to local instances and systems of racial injustice. The week before our congregation joined with African-American churches to march in prayer and protest after our worship services, I emailed a few other pastors in our city to invite them to participate. One predominantly white congregation on the other side of the city decided to join us. But rather than leave their mostly white neighborhood to come to our community, they decided to take to the sidewalks outside their sanctuary. In front of their white neighbors, this congregation demonstrated their solidarity with their African-American family on the other end of the city. In doing so, they collectively proclaimed the gospel of the kingdom to neighbors and passersby who would not have otherwise been aware of the racial injustices that impact many of their fellow citizens in our segregated city.

A public protest should not be mistaken for verbally sharing the gospel, but corporate moments like this allow a white church to experience the power of representing the kingdom of God together. As we've noted, one of the significant challenges of discipling white Christians away from segregation is that we do not consciously identify ourselves as a racial group. We don't consciously think of ourselves as white. But by emphasizing how a white church can bear witness to the kingdom together, the practice of evangelism can reveal the importance of claiming our shared, if fraught, identity.

NEARNESS

Another way to reimagine evangelism is to emphasize the nearness of the kingdom of God. The disembodied and detached view of individual salvation common in many white churches might provide a future hope, but it does little to empower believers for lives of discipleship in the here and now. The danger is compounded for white Christians who, having been societally discipled into deceptive privilege, are often left in a false contentment. We do not sense the urgency felt by many Christians of color who viscerally experience the yawning gap between the righteousness of the kingdom and our nation's many injustices.

All of this begins to change when we start paying attention to how often Jesus talked about the kingdom of God. His consistent announcements of the availability of God's reign through his own presence was good news to those with ears to hear and eyes to see. The kingdom is near because our King has come near. It is not a future spiritual reality for us to wait for—though we do wait expectantly for its consummation—but a present and available realm for us to enter right now.

There is a huge difference between a gospel that focuses mostly on the future and one that invites people to experience and represent God's reign today. Though we should never lose our hopeful orientation toward the future—it has been the anchor for many oppressed Christians over the generations—we must show how that future hope is even now expressed by our orientation into the available kingdom of God.

A community of white Christians who are being equipped to share the good news of the nearby kingdom will notice things we previously missed. Take for example the racial disparities in the criminal justice system. Though the system seems to "work" for many white citizens, its inequities are keenly felt throughout communities of color. While African Americans are no more likely to commit a crime than white people, they are five times more likely to be imprisoned.[6] Authors like Michelle Alexander and Dominque Gilliard have documented the devastating impact our unjust criminal justice system has not only on individuals but also on their families and communities.[7]

As white Christians begin looking for evidence of the nearby kingdom of God, we will begin to discover the many ways God's reign of righteousness is opposed by our racialized society. Of course, until the return of King Jesus, the kingdoms of this earth will always rebel against his rule. The relevant point here is that white Christians have often been blind to this rebellion, interpreting our own relative comfort and security as evidence of God's blessing. But as a white church begins inviting people not to individualistic salvation but into a life of discipleship in the kingdom of God, its members will have to reckon with these blind spots. This reckoning, while painful, can lead to much greater solidarity with those who've suffered under the weight of our racial privilege.

But there is another side to this. Recently I was listening to one of our church's members, an African-American woman, describe her childhood church experience. She recalled fondly the testimonies shared almost every Sunday, remembering how both adults and children would stand to share specific ways that God had provided for and protected them throughout the week. And then, in a quieter voice, she said, "We needed those testimonies." Within a culture that often opposed them, the members of this small black church experienced these words of witness as evidence of God's presence among them. The kingdom was near.

As white Christians become closer with Christians of color, we will become better interpreters of the presence of the kingdom among us. After all, despite suffering our society's racism and white supremacist assumptions, our siblings of color can still testify to the evidence of God's kingdom. Over time, we too will develop the eyes to see with greater clarity as we invite others to join in following Jesus into the kingdom he has made available.

INVITATION

Having grasped the corporate nature of evangelism as we learn to see and announce the nearness of the kingdom, we can intentionally invite white people to become Jesus' disciples. Rather than simply asking people to accept Jesus as their personal (individualistic) savior, it "must be our conscious objective, consciously implemented, to bring others to the point where they are daily learning from Jesus how to live their actual lives as he would live them if he were they."[8] Hopefully by now the distinction is clear. As Christ's ambassadors of his reconciliation, we invite people to follow Jesus, to become like Jesus in order to do what

Jesus does. The point about purposefulness is especially relevant for us. As white Christians begin understanding the impact of racial whiteness and privilege on all white people, we will engage prayerfully and intentionally with the call to make disciples of white people.

I realize that even now the idea of identifying the race of those we are called to make disciples of—*white* people—will sound grating to some of us. And certainly white Christians should not only invite other white people to become disciples. But most white people are more likely to hear the difficult truths about the sins related to privilege and supremacy from other white people. This is our responsibility. Michael Eric Dyson, in a charge to white people, makes this point plainly.

> You must school your white brothers and sisters, your cousins and uncles, your loved ones and friends, and all who will listen to you. . . . Share with them what you learn about us, but share as well what you learn about yourself, about how whiteness works. You see, my friends, there is only so much I can say to white folk, only so much they can hear from me or anyone who isn't white.[9]

But how do we go about intentionally inviting white people to become disciples of Jesus? It can be complicated. I have seen many white Christians early on in their second conversions to racial justice get overwhelmed by how much they need to learn. Not wanting to make a mistake or say something ignorant sounding, these well-meaning learners simply keep their mouths shut.

While it's important for white Christians to continue growing in our awareness of the histories and current realities our privilege has concealed from us, these things should never keep us from making disciples. Thankfully, Jesus himself gives us an accessible pattern when he sends his disciples before he ascends into heaven: "But you will receive power when the Holy Spirit comes on you; and you will be my witnesses in Jerusalem, and in all Judea and Samaria, and to the ends of the earth" (Acts 1:8).

"Witness," writes pastor and author John Teter, "is not a side issue in the life of Jesus' disciples. It is *the* issue! It is the only difference between one person rejecting Jesus and another worshiping him."[10] With Dyson's practical wisdom in our ears, we can see the importance of this essential aspect of discipleship being intentionally addressed to white people. After all, who better to bear witness to the power of Jesus to rescue white people from the grip of privilege and supremacy than other white people who have themselves been rescued?

IMITATION

Finally, as the white church begins holding together evangelism and justice, we can choose to follow the example of the American black church. As a whole, this Christian tradition has long held together gospel proclamation and justice.

As a white church intentionally invites people to follow Jesus into his nearby kingdom, it will benefit from reaching out to a local African-American church, or any congregation of color with a cohesive vision of evangelism and justice. Perhaps this other church would allow a small team of white leaders to volunteer at one of their outreach events. Or maybe a few members of the white church would be sent as guests to the black church for a season to listen carefully for how the gospel is proclaimed to that community. What does the gospel of the kingdom *sound* like? How are members and guests invited to respond? While these may sound like overly simple suggestions, those of us without an imagination for this sort of evangelism will benefit greatly from this exposure.

A few years ago I received a phone call from a white pastor who wanted to talk about a special service his church was planning to address some of the disturbing instances of racism then in the news. Along with recounting that there would be a time for prayer and lament, he told me that one of the few African American members of the church would be sharing some of his experiences with racism with the mostly white congregation. He wondered if I had any suggestions as he finished planning the service.

In conversations like this one I have two initial internal responses. First, I'm so thankful that a white church is taking intentional steps to address racial injustice. When white pastors or ministry leaders take the step to lead in this direction, they are stepping into uncharted territory.

It requires courage to face the potential pushback from some and it's always encouraging to see leaders who are willing to face the cost. The other response I had during that phone call was a lament. While I understood why this white pastor was reaching out to me, another white pastor, how much more helpful would a conversation have been with a trusted pastor of color?

As we begin to identify more closely with our siblings of color, and especially the African-American church, we can imagine that same pastor, planning that important service, but with a small network of friends and colleagues of color who he could reach out to. What, he might ask, would they want him to remember? How could he to the best of his ability represent their concerns and hopes before his own church? With this cloud of witnesses filling his imagination, this faithful and courageous white pastor could embody a holistic gospel—word and deed—before the people he has been called to disciple.

■ ■ ■

What could happen if a white church reimagined evangelism as a discipleship practice? For starters, I believe many white people would be reached with a gospel that reconciles them with their Creator as well as across lines of cultural and racial division. What a powerful testimony to our racialized society that would be! But also, the members of that congregation would find themselves being led to greater harmony with their Christian siblings of color. Through the abundance of the kingdom of God, by intentionally discipling *white* people into the kingdom, white Christians will find themselves growing beyond their segregation to the reconciliation of the body of Christ.

CHAPTER TEN

PRACTICING UNCOMMON FRIENDSHIP

THE APPROACH WE HAVE TAKEN in these pages to address racial injustice and segregation is in one very important regard different from how racial reconciliation has typically been pursued by white Christians. If we are concerned at all about race, we have tended to think about the problem of racial injustice and segregation as one of relational separation, of different racial and ethnic groups being distanced from one another such that the unity of the church is compromised. From this perspective, the obvious solution is to bridge the separation and bring formerly divided people together. Multiethnic and multiracial relationships are the evidence of success in this version of racial reconciliation.

This model of reconciliation prioritizes the comfort of white people over the well-being of people of color. By elevating reconciled relationships, white people are not asked to grapple with the nature and impact of our own whiteness. We don't have to think about the way race, as a way of identifying and categorizing people, was intentionally constructed over time as a means to benefit some while exploiting others. Neither do we have to acknowledge the material realities of racial injustice and segregation. If cross-racial relationships are the goal, then as long as I can point to a couple friends of color, I don't have to notice how race makes the lived realities of those same friends far more difficult than my own.

Not only does a relational model of reconciliation privilege my own comfort, it also plugs my ears when its inadequacies are pointed out. Remember the people of color who joined mostly white churches that voiced a commitment to racial reconciliation? These women and men were drawn to the vision of genuine community across lines of segregation and division and, for a time, they felt welcomed. But during moments of public racial trauma—a case of police brutality or a politician stoking racial animus—these people of color turned to their new white acquaintances for solidarity, only to be met with silence. Or they were discouraged from bringing up so-called political issues in church. The white church members were content simply to have people of color in their church and to be in relationship with them. Because success had been defined as moving from separation to togetherness, they were unwilling to hear the pressing concerns expressed by their sisters and brothers of color.

Again, our approach has been purposefully different. From the limitations of our own racial whiteness, we are attempting to prioritize the well-being of people of color over our own white comfort. We have done this first of all by framing the problem of race not as separation but as injustice.

Appealing to a modicum of racial diversity in our white churches or to our own personal friends of color as evidence of racial reconciliation is overly optimistic and detached from reality. Such reconciliation can be accomplished without ever acknowledging, much less addressing, the underlying reasons for racial and ethnic divisions. White people are left feeling good about what has been achieved while everyone else remains exposed to racism and white supremacy.

When relational togetherness is the goal of a reconciliation model, each distinct racial or ethnic group is thought about similarly. Everyone, regardless of race or ethnicity, is called to overcome the barriers that keep us apart. In this regard as well, our approach is different. We have identified racial whiteness as a social and historical construct that still influences our society. We are focused on the particularities of whiteness and the subsequent responsibilities white Christians have to address racial segregation and injustice. For white people, acknowledging our

racial whiteness and its associated privileges and assumptions of superiority is hard work indeed. As we've seen, race as it has been constructed and evolved works to conceal its impact *on* white people *from*
white people. Our imaginations and assumptions have been discipled
by our racialized society not to think of ourselves in racial terms. For
most of us, white is neutral.

But it's not. Race is a construction intended to have material impact
in the world by elevating those of us who came to see ourselves as white.
So any attempt to elevate the well-being of people of color over the
comfort of white people must grapple with whiteness. The model I'm
advocating does not expect everyone to do the same kind of work.
Rather, white Christians must undergo a particular kind of discipleship
that addresses our own peculiar responsibilities for racial injustice and
segregation, including how our complicity has privileged us at the expense of our siblings in Christ.

By prioritizing racial justice over relational togetherness, and by
accounting for the particularities of whiteness, our reimagined discipleship practices can address the characteristics of white Christianity
that typically inhibit attempts at racial reconciliation: namely individualism, relationalism, and antistructuralism. Counterintuitive as this
approach will be to most white Christians, pursuing it courageously will
offer us the real possibility of escaping the dead ends in which we have
found ourselves. No matter how diverse or not we find our churches or
neighborhoods to be, this approach allows each of us to meaningfully
address racial segregation and injustice. Moving away from a relational
model with its logic in a half-told reality allows white churches to jump
into the work of reconciliation meant to be an inherent part of our
Christian identity.

■ ■ ■

In this book I have repeatedly prioritized racial justice over relational
reconciliation; it might seem that the implication is that racially reconciled relationships are not all that important. And, in fact, some who
advocate similar approaches to racial justice appear to hold little regard
for cross-racial relationships. For some, these relationships are not

something to pursue but are believed to be something that will develop eventually as a result of pursuing racial justice. While I understand this perspective, I am convinced that any *Christian* attempt to address racial injustice and segregation must also prioritize relationships across lines of division.

I have put this chapter at the end because it is important to frame these relationships within the overall pursuit of justice, especially given our persistent tendency to prioritize individual relationships at the expense of the material realities of racism. Still, ours is a journey to solidarity with the racially and ethnically diverse body of Christ, so flesh and blood relationships must be a part of this journey. Though it's possible that these relationships will develop as a result of increasing instances of racial justice, it's imperative that we intentionally nurture these relationships even as we prioritize racial justice. Why? The reasons have to do with the embodied nature of solidarity, the blind spots of whiteness, the difference made by proximity, and a Christian understanding of friendship.

■ ■ ■

Theologian Brian Bantum says that race is a de-creating system.[1] It detaches us from the places that God intended to form us and disembodies us such that we do not feel our divinely designed need for one another. In an ironic twist, from the confines of our racially discipled imaginations, fighting for justice for people of color without also pursuing relationships with some of those same people could leave this de-creating (detaching, disembodying) attribute of race largely undisturbed. In other words, it is possible to seek justice *for* someone without being in relationship *with* them.

Solidarity, though, requires embodied relationships. We cannot seek justice for an idea or a principle. Our efforts must align with the goals that have been articulated by women and men of color; otherwise we will succumb to what our racialized imaginations assume is best for people we've never met.

Another reason to pursue cross-racial relationships as we address racial injustices is that white people cannot be trusted to understand how our whiteness deceives us. When Wendell Berry looked over his life, he realized that he had learned more about his own racial identity from two black childhood friends than from any white person. "[In] the effort to live meaningfully and decently in America," he wrote, "a white man simply cannot learn all that he needs to know from other American white men."[2]

Almost everything I know about how race has impacted me has come from friends, mentors, pastors, and authors of color. Lifelong friends like Michael Washington, spiritual directors like Debbie Blue, mentors like Brenda Salter McNeil, neighborhood pastors like Chris Harris, Michael Neal, L. Bernard Jakes, and Michelle Dodson, along with the women and men of color in our church, have each shown me more about myself than I'd have ever learned within segregated white spaces. They have had to understand whiteness in a way that white people never have to grasp. The impact of my racial privilege is dramatically different on me than on my friends of color: I am distracted and deceived by it, led to believe that my successes are solely due to my work ethic and dedication; they are awakened by it, alerted to the ways distracted power wreaks terrible havoc on vulnerable people.

If the damaging isolation of segregation is one reason to pursue cross-racial relationships, the potential benefit of proximity is its opposite. Experiencing meaningful solidarity with Christians of color requires that I actually be in relationship with at least some of those same people. In the context of these friendships, my ears will slowly be unstopped and my eyes opened. In place of the echo chamber of segregation, we will have access to creative possibilities in the journey toward solidarity that never would have otherwise presented themselves.

It's important to note that the quality of proximity white people have to people of color matters. Simply having a friend or two of color is not enough to bring white people into solidarity with people of color. As Emerson and Smith point out, a white person's entire social network must be proximate with people of color in order for that person's perspective to be challenged and changed.[3] This is the important difference between the simplistic relationalism common to much of white

Christianity and a holistic sort of intertwining relationships that make a genuine difference in how white people see the world.

I have experienced this hopeful dynamic time after time as I sit in conversations with our church's racially diverse staff. As we wrestle with difficult and sensitive topics, I am always amazed at the paths that open up as I shut my mouth and listen. It's not that I can't contribute to these critical conversations. Rather, I have learned over the years to notice the limits of my racially discipled imagination and to be curious about what God has for his church beyond those limits. It's always good!

Lastly, pursuing relationships alongside justice is important because of how important friendship is within Christianity. In the Gospel of John, Jesus tells his disciples, "Greater love has no one than this: to lay down one's life for one's friends" (John 15:13). It's significant that the image Jesus chose to express God's sacrificial love comes from the kind of relationships that prioritize a friend's needs above my own. In the context of the New Testament church, we must imagine these friendships from the perspective of the surrounding culture. Christian friendship crossed boundaries of gender, class, culture, language, and ethnicity. There was nothing normal about these friendships that pointed to God's love for his people.

Ensuring that cross-racial friendships are a part of how we address racial injustice and segregation is a way to be faithful to how Christians have lived into our oneness in Christ. Our unity has never been simply a matter of belief or a hoped-for reality after Christ's return. Rather, the early Christians understood that their present relationships across divisions were evidence of the comprehensive reconciliation accomplished by Jesus on the cross.

Because the problem we are addressing is not relational separateness but material injustice, our goal is not relational reconciliation. But pursuing cross-racial reconciling relationships must be a part of any Christian strategy to address racial injustice and segregation. Brenda Salter McNeil defines reconciliation as "an ongoing spiritual process involving forgiveness, repentance and justice that restores broken relationships and systems to reflect God's original intention for all creation to flourish."[4] While Salter McNeil understands the importance of highlighting unjust systems, she also sees the place for relationships that have been restored via forgiveness, repentance, and justice. So while maintaining the emphases on racial injustice and the particularities of whiteness, we can also reimagine cross-racial friendships as one of our discipleship practices.

■ ■ ■

Before getting to specific ways the practice of friendship can disciple white Christians away from racial injustice and segregation, it's worth asking whether such friendships exist in most white churches. After all, it's our goal to take current practices and reimagine them for the journey toward solidarity. Given the extent of our segregation, we need to look hard for the possibilities of cross-racial friendships in white Christianity.

It has been my experience that many white churches value cross-cultural missions. Much of this work takes place in other countries while some happens closer—in a nearby city, for example. A common theme when it comes to cross-cultural missions is the relationships that can develop between a white church and those they serve. So, on some level at least, there exists a precedent for cross-racial relationships in many white churches.

Still, most of these relationships exist because white Christians decide to serve their new cross-cultural friends in some capacity. There is an inherent power dynamic to these relationships that allows white Christians to set agendas, ministry priorities, and project timelines. This instinct to serve cross-culturally, with its associated assumptions about power and control, needs to mature into solidarity with the racially diverse body of Christ.

The difference is important. Whereas relationships born out of service often perpetuate existing unequal power dynamics, Christian solidarity aims at relational mutuality. As Sandra Van Opstal notes, Christians "stand with one another, as communities and individuals, in lament that leads to hope. We rejoice with one another when we see glimpses of the power of the gospel transforming situations."[5] This is an experience between friends, in which each person can come with their needs and resources, with their fears and hopes. Relationships born from the commitment to solidarity allow for those of us who are white to hear uncomfortable truths about ourselves from friends of color, truths that our power and privilege typically shield us from.

So as we reimagine cross-racial relationships as a discipleship practice, we are keeping in mind our aim of solidarity along with our commitments to address racial injustice and the particularities of whiteness. With these guardrails in place, we can highlight the importance of reconciled relationships without losing our way in the journey toward racial justice. To help us stay this narrow course, I have included short testimonies from a few white friends. In their own ways, each of them embodies how cross-racial friendships can disciple us toward solidarity. They have helped me see how to pursue these relationships as white people who are committed to racial justice.

MATURITY

For friendship to be a discipleship practice, we must begin with our own relational maturity. We have seen how our racialized society disciples white people toward fragility that often crumbles when confronted with difficult truths about ourselves. When encountering chapters of our nation's history that we had previously overlooked—massacres of Native Americans, racial terror inflicted on newly freed African-American citizens, corrupt voting laws that racially discriminate—we often get overwhelmed and turn away. Or when we discover how our racial privilege has attracted unearned benefits, we often choose to debate the facts rather than empathize with the consequences on people of color.

In his book about white identity, pastor Daniel Hill identifies some stages that many white people go through as they awaken to realities of racial injustice.[6] Denial, disorientation, shame, and self-righteousness are all natural emotional experiences in this process. Too many of us, however, get stuck in these places. Rather than growing in our emotional capacity to respond to new information and experiences, we remain caught in a kind of spiritual immaturity. It seems we would prefer to shield ourselves from hard truths than walk the painful road toward solidarity.

During the inevitable times of disorientation that white people will face as we grow in our racial awareness, our tendency will be to retreat

Bret Widman, Director of the CRUX program, North Park University's Christian discipleship living-learning program where incoming freshmen live in community for a year

How has the trajectory of your ministry been impacted by the women and men of color who have discipled you over the years?

I grew up in a small, rural, white community of 250 people and was the first person in my family to get a college education; it was at college that I began to follow Jesus for the first time. That said, one of the most transformational educations I have benefited from has been being intentionally discipled by people of color.

This choice changed the way I read Scripture. I had already graduated from two excellent seminaries and had served in the local church for years. Yet I had never considered my own lenses as I approached the Word of God. Through those that discipled me, I began to see things in the text that I had never noticed before. Not only did my preaching change but the application as well. I began to better understand this kingdom that Jesus taught, gave examples of, and invited people to participate in. I am indebted to the formation I have received from my brothers and sisters who courageously helped me become more like Jesus. Without their input, I never would have become aware of my own blindness.

to the known comforts of our segregated lives. But Hill points out that we can instead choose to persist as we experience confusing disruptions to our assumptions about the world and ourselves. "The resilient person *recovers from* disruption. The resilient person *persists through* disruption. The resilient person even learns to *thrive amid* disruption."[7]

For friendship to become a discipleship practice, we white Christians must grow in our resiliency toward maturity. I have found that preaching can be one of the times to encourage this resiliency. Because our multiracial church regularly addresses racial injustice and white supremacy from a variety of angles, I am aware of the confusion some of the newer white people might be experiencing. While it's common for racism and its impact to be addressed in many of the black churches in our neighborhood, for many of our white people it's a brand new—and disorienting!—experience.

Yet rather than leaving people in their confusion, I will often act as the commentator on my own sermon. I'm not sure when I started doing this, but it may have been after watching the sitcom *Arrested Development*. In that absurd TV show about a wealthy, clueless, and incredibly selfish family, the voice of producer Ron Howard often interrupts to clarify, contextualize, or correct something that was just said by one of the actors. In the framework of the show, it's a funny trick to call out the characters' constant lies. I sometimes do a similar thing when preaching some especially difficult truth having to do with race. I will pause, step away from the pulpit, and say something like, "Look, I know for some of us, especially those of us who are white, the experience of talking about race in church can be pretty jarring. At our church we discuss these difficult realties regularly because we believe the gospel calls us to be a reconciled people who address racial injustice. But that can be a challenge if you've never thought about how race has impacted you or the person sitting next to you. I encourage you to sit with your confusion, anger, grief, or whatever else you are feeling. Don't distract yourself from it. And if you want to talk about what you're feeling or what you're hearing today, please find me after the service."

By simply acknowledging what white people are feeling as they are confronted with disorienting truths, we can build their resiliency and lead them toward maturity. As white Christians mature, we become less self-defensive about race. Instead, our emotional capacity grows to include loving curiosity about the experiences of our Christian siblings as well as empathy when learning how our racialized society has impacted them. The more mature we become, the better friends we will be.

IDENTIFY

Another way for friendships to become a discipleship practice is for white Christians to identify with Christians of color. Sandra Van Opstal points out that the "words *reconciliation* and *exchange* share the same root (e.g., money being exchanged in equal value). In reconciliation, we

Rev. Luke Swanson, pastor in North Minneapolis whose church is a worshiping, reconciling, community-empowering, discipling movement seeking to bless an often-neglected neighborhood. He is the only white lead pastor in his historic African-American neighborhood.

How has your posture of submission to the spiritual authority of African-American clergy impacted your discipleship?

This work is messy but thick with the presence of God and the joy of the Lord. Because of the nature of sin, reconciliation work should never be done alone but needs a Christ-centered body. I am thankful for my black sisters and brothers who have walked with me in this journey, not only affirming me as a Christian brother in the faith, but also confronting me where my whiteness has blinded me to see how my actions have alienated or hurt others. What I have learned has often come through mistakes and a community that told me the truth while also clothing me with grace and not kicking me to the curb.

Submitting to the authority of others is a communal act, at times painfully self-reflective, and always deeply spiritual. I remember being discouraged in this work one season when an African-American mother of the church said, "Pastor, if no one is ever upset or mad at you, you're doing something wrong." Her words reminded me that this work requires us to stay in the tension and not run. Although Jesus keeps me in ministry, my friendships and partnerships with clergy and colleagues, particularly clergy of color, always seem to tie the knot of faith and keep me from letting go.

exchange perspectives or change places."[8] On an essential level, white Christians must come to see ourselves, including the priorities for our lives and ministries, in the embodied experiences of Christians of color.

Does this sound too simplistic? After all, a fundamental trait of Christian faith is that we are each bound to one another in Christ. No matter our differences, what we share in common through Jesus is what matters the most. While that's theologically accurate, and few

Christians of any race or ethnicity would disagree, we have seen that white Christians often practically share more in common with white non-Christians than we do with Christians of color. Our assumptions and decisions are more predictable by race than faith in large part because we do not identify ourselves with the larger body of Christ.

One simple way to begin relationally identifying beyond segregation is for church leaders to diversify the books they read, the authors and scholars they cite, and the examples and illustrations they use. Voices of color can then be naturally integrated into the rhythms of preaching and worship so that they become a part of the chorus forming the church. This means referring to an Asian-American biblical scholar in a sermon, sharing a story (with permission) from the Latino/a church down the street, or inviting a black preacher to the white church's pulpit on a Sunday that is *not* during Black History Month or on Martin Luther King Jr. Day weekend.

Perhaps that last example seems odd. As a white church intentionally expands the racially diverse voices influencing it, it is important to balance two dynamics. The first is the tendency toward colorblindness. A white church must grow in its ability to see and welcome these diverse voices in a way that values their full humanity, including their racial, ethnic, and cultural particularities. The other tendency to avoid is the one that stereotypes people of color to specific, racially constrained issues, such as always including a black preacher on Martin Luther King weekend. This communicates to white people that the expertise of people of color is limited to obvious racial issues while everything else can be adequately handled by white people.

By avoiding colorblindness and stereotyping, we can begin more authentically identifying across our segregation. White Christians will participate in their churches and find that, despite the narrative of racial difference at work on us by our society, we are beginning to imagine ourselves as members of the body of Christ. One result of this growing imagination is that white Christians can more easily identify with Christians of color. We can see our siblings in their particularities, though not bound to them stereotypically in the manner our racialized society would have us imagine.

FRIENDSHIP

Dr. Brandy Liebscher, psychologist, educator, and founder of Facing Ourselves, an organization dedicated to equipping and mobilizing white Christians to combat racial injustice and create systemic change

How have your friendships with people of color impacted your engagement with systems of racial injustice?

In an effort to truly understand the realities of racism, I've read many books and watched countless documentaries. Did I learn a lot from those resources? Yes, I did. However, an intellectual understanding of systemic racism alone could never have been enough to give me the courage to fight against the systemic injustice people of color endure every day.

My friendships with people of color changed all that. As I began to witness firsthand the impact of systemic racism in their lives—something I had never experienced as a white person—what had begun as an intellectual understanding evolved into something deeper. Rather than simply ask, "What is racism?" I began to ask, "How do I stand up and fight systemic injustice?" This is another way of asking, "How do I lay down my life for my friend?" It is a question that for me was birthed from community, friendship, and ultimately, kinship. This has been what has most motivated and inspired me to fight systemic injustice.

If maturity and identification are the groundwork for cross-racial friendships, at some point white people must intentionally make friends with people of color. Does this sound strange? Maybe even wrong? Perhaps it should. As I talk with white Christian leaders who are waking up to their own segregated lives, I often hear something like, "Well, what am I supposed to do? Walk up to some random person of color and ask them to be my friend?" Obviously, the answer to this sarcastic question is no. Please never, ever do that. The other side of this are the friends of color who've shared with me how tiring it is to be a white person's lone friend of color. I've listened sadly as they've shared how exhausting it is to constantly be explaining race and racism only to have their lived experience debated and written off. For a person of color, the experience of being a white person's friend all too often becomes an exercise in justifying their own existence.

So let's acknowledge that when we're talking about purposefully pursuing cross-racial friendships we want to stay far away from either of these dynamics. But let's also acknowledge the danger of *not* pursuing these friendships. As Michael Eric Dyson laments, "Not knowing black folk intimately exacerbates the distance between the white self and the black other."[9] Indeed, such is the nature of our segregation that the lack of friendships serves to reinforce it. So, Dyson urges, white people must "set out immediately to find and make friends with black folks who share their interests. It's not as hard as it seems. Black folk come in every variety of belief, ideology, and politics, just as any other American does, and the vast majority of us are morally upright."[10]

Dyson is being slightly sarcastic to make a point: making cross-racial friends may not be as hard as some of us have thought. True, there are complicating factors such as the ones we have identified, but especially for a congregation that is being intentional, these can be mitigated and relational possibilities opened up. I can personally attest that the close friendships I have with people of color began simply by stumbling into areas of shared affinity. (It's probably not surprising that many of these friends are also pastors!)

The challenge, of course, is that the nature of societal segregation and the segregation of our churches means that many white Christians never see the opportunities to pursue these relationships. How can we expect to begin nurturing friendships if we are never even around people of color? This is where the church becomes so important. By planning events— worship services, service projects, missions trips—with churches of color, a white church is creating one of the *only* spaces that many white Christians will have to meaningfully engage with racially and ethnically diverse people.

Let's imagine a white church that has over time been intentional about discipling its people toward spiritual maturity and has helped them personally identify with the racially diverse body of Christ. The leaders of this church have also been developing a relationship with a nearby Latino/a church, comprising first-generation Spanish-speaking immigrants and a younger English-speaking generation. Perhaps they have worshiped together once or twice, singing in both languages, translating the sermon so that all can participate. The leaders from both churches have noticed that during the summer many elementary-age kids in the community don't have many opportunities for structured recreation and creative expression, so, after much planning, the two churches agree to offer a one-week sports and arts camp that will offer programming in English and Spanish. The camp will meet real needs as identified by the community, but it will take a lot of people power to pull it off.

All of the previously laid relational groundwork now comes into play as these two churches—very different when it comes to culture, ethnicity, and even language—work side by side to care for their community. Far from being a one-off outreach event, service project, or missions trip, this summer camp provides the shared relational space for members of both congregations to begin building friendships. Because the leaders of these churches understand how important these budding friendships are to their Christian identity, they end the program with a joint worship service and potluck on the Sunday after the camp. Testimonies are shared and phone numbers exchanged. Three months later everyone is invited to a Friday evening dinner where a video of highlights from the camp is shown, and time is given for members of both churches to share about how they are nurturing their new cross-cultural friendships.

I realize that this might sound like a lot of work. Maybe it sounds more like social planning and less like typical church ministry. But once a white church grasps the importance of friendship as a discipleship practice, while also realizing how impossible these friendships will seem to many white Christians, choosing to create friendship-nurturing spaces can become a natural part of ministry.

REPAIR

A final way to reimagine friendship as a practice for solidarity is to prioritize repair. Our focus on justice does not allow us to be content with the mere existence of cross-racial friendships. These friendships need to show how white Christians are committed to working alongside our friends to repair what has been damaged by racial injustice and segregation.

Prioritizing repair does not mean that white Christians decide what needs to be fixed. By now we are aware of the inadequacy of our ability to diagnose what is wrong in our racialized society, much less describe how it might be fixed. Rather, friendships aimed at solidarity allow white Christians to join the righteous work of repair that has long been a part of many churches of color. This won't be simple. "Repair," writes Harvey, "offers no easy answers, nor any final solutions (most cases of racial atrocity in the United States can never be truly repaired)."[11]

Even so, by joining our siblings in Christ in their efforts to right what has been marred by racial injustice and white supremacy, our growing awareness can be translated into actions that respond materially to the damage done by segregation and injustice. More often than not, white churches will not need to start new programs to effectively address racial injustice. There are already many churches and ministries of color that have long been demonstrating the justice of the kingdom of God through specific initiatives, partnerships, and programs. Often these churches have found willing partners in government and the nonprofit sector, even as white churches have remained uninterested. But as white Christians nurture cross-racial friendships, we will become aware of these already-existing opportunities. We can then accept the invitations of these new friends to bring whatever resources and networks we have to these various expressions of repair.

In my own city there are organizations advocating for criminal justice reform, humane immigration policies, and changes to how public education is funded. Other groups help low-income families secure tax returns that are often unclaimed, advocate for communities suffering from toxic chemicals from nearby waste-treatment facilities, and assist first-generation college students navigating the complexities of admission and financial aid. Focusing on repair does not mean that we totally fix the sources of racial injustice; the problems are deeply entrenched and the spiritual opposition is great. But from our place within networks of racially diverse friends, we can align our efforts with the kingdom of God that shines into even the deepest shadows. Joining our friends to repair the damages of racial injustice and segregation *is* solidarity.

■ ■ ■

I chose to end this survey of reimagined discipleship practices with friendship for a very personal reason. While the journey from segregation to solidarity is lifelong and often costly, the experience of friendship constantly reminds me of just how *good* it is. I share good meals with my friends. I laugh long and loud with them. I've entrusted my children to my friends, and they've done the same with Maggie and me. I've traveled with my friends, faced frightening circumstances with them, and reminisced with them about the miraculous things we've seen God do in our church and city.

To be honest, I cannot accurately understand myself outside the embrace of my friends. It is evidence of the extravagant grace of God that I can call these women and men my friends and that they would claim me as their own.

CONCLUSION

I HAVE MANY WONDERFUL MEMORIES of the white churches that nurtured my faith, from my earliest years following my mother's finger as she traced the words we sang from battered hymnbooks, to memorizing Bible verses in Sunday School, to the weekend men's trips in high school when my dad and I would drive across the border with Mexico to help local churches build houses for those living amidst poverty. My more recent experiences in multiracial congregations cause me to look back on some of those memories critically, but I cannot help but feel immense gratitude for the saints who consistently pointed me to Jesus.

One of the favorite verses in the churches of my childhood was the well-known passage: "And do not be conformed to this world, but be transformed by the renewing of your mind, that you may prove what is that good and acceptable and perfect will of God" (Romans 12:2 NKJV). Paul's words were a regular reminder that what was normal in the world was not to be normal for us. We had been saved into the family of God and were to live as salt and light, to bear witness to God's good, acceptable, and perfect will.

In these churches we often identified important ways we were not to conform to the world, but I cannot remember ever hearing a call to resist the worldly patterns of racial injustice and segregation. Inasmuch as we thought about these things, we assumed that our churches' racial divisions were the natural result of individual and cultural preferences. When we did attempt to cross those boundaries, it was with the desire to experience closer relationships with our fellow Christians. The idea of addressing racial injustices, much less our own complicity with those injustices as white people, was never a part of what we imagined for our discipleship.

But our segregation was not normal, and it certainly was not benign. Though I didn't know it then, the historical construction of race functioned to privilege the members of our white churches while inflicting material harm on our siblings of color. Our own imaginations and assumptions were being discipled away from the reconciled kingdom of God, and our churches were unwilling to call us back.

That we were willfully ignorant of these facts did not make them any less true. We had been conformed to this world. We had conformed to our society's patterns of racial injustice and segregation. Sadly, this has been the tendency of the white American church as long as there have been white Christians in this country.

It is past time for white churches to make disciples of Jesus who do not conform to our racialized society. It's not more diversity we need; it's better discipleship that calls white Christians to follow Jesus into the kingdom of God. This is a kingdom of reconciliation, patterned on the righteous reconciliation won for the world by Jesus' death and resurrection. It is a kingdom that prioritizes justice and that reckons seriously with how we have been deformed by the society's narrative of racial difference.

Because we are desiring beings who navigate this world imaginatively, it is possible to begin discipling white Christians away from segregation right now. We don't have to wait for racial and cultural diversity to increase some day in the future. We don't have to outsource the call to racial justice to urban churches or multiracial congregations. We can do this good work right now, wherever we find ourselves. The reimagined discipleship practices in the previous chapters are not comprehensive. I hope you've thought of additional possibilities already! But they are a place to begin the journey to solidarity.

It can be overwhelming to consider the depth and breadth of the racialized discipleship that has aimed us away from the body of Christ. But consider the possibilities as well. While our culture increasingly touts multiculturalism and racial diversity, recent years have shown the extent to which we remain segregated from one another and how rampant racial injustice remains.

Imagine, then, a white church that purposefully, humbly, and courageously pursues a new course—a nonconforming course. Imagine a white church making disciples of white Christians who are finding their way to embodied solidarity with Christians of color. Imagine ecclesial unity that is not simply proclaimed as a theological truth or experienced at an occasional event but that becomes the lived, enfleshed realities for white Christians. Imagine a community of white Christians that cannot be categorized or understood without accounting for their friends of color. Imagine if race was a less accurate predictor of political perspective than the testimonies of the racially diverse beloved body of Christ. Imagine if pollsters could no longer categorize white Christians by their race because it was no longer an adequate predictor of who we vote for, or whose partisan policies we support.

I'm under no delusion about just how unlikely this vision is. Racial discipleship has powerfully formed our imaginations. Our assumptions have been profoundly warped by the discipleship of a racialized society. The walls of segregation that we have built seem impenetrable.

But the kingdom of God, Jesus said, is like yeast: just a little is needed to work its way all through the dough. It's like a barely visible mustard seed, which grows to give shelter to many birds. And so, despite the evidence of the past, I am daring to imagine a different future. I hope you will too.

ACKNOWLEDGMENTS

This book wouldn't exist if not for Helen Lee's hunch that I might have something to say. She and a few others believed in me long before I did. My editor at InterVarsity Press, Ethan McCarthy, asked the right questions at the right times to keep this project grounded in reality.

New Community Covenant Church insisted that I take my sabbatical when I tried to put it off, which gave me time to dig into the questions that eventually became this book. After ten years, I'm still grateful that I get to pastor this church for whom Christ's reconciliation is a vision wide and deep enough to give our lives.

My friends and colleagues Pastors Chris Harris, Michael Neal, and L. Bernard Jakes welcomed me to the neighborhood and have discipled me in more ways than I'll ever know. I hope this book can be some small evidence of my gratitude for their presence and leadership.

My imagination for the possibilities expressed in these pages owes so much to the spiritual direction of Rev. Debbie Blue, the mentorship of Rev. Dr. Brenda Salter McNeil, and the friendship of Rev. Michael Washington. My fellow pastor Michelle Dodson and her husband, Karlos, consistently remind me that *nothing* is impossible with God. Derek Boggs, Kimberly Whetstone, Won Kim, and others mentioned here read an early draft of this book and their suggestions and critique were in valuable.

The centrality of discipleship for the ministry of racial reconciliation came into focus during a series of rich conversations with a group of pastors and leaders from around the country. José Humphreys, Brandy Liebscher, Luke Swanson, Liz Mosbo VerHage, Rob Fairbanks, Bret Widman, and Daniel Hill each helped me understand the generally overlooked intersection of racial justice and discipleship to Jesus.

I'm exceedingly grateful for family members who love me despite my introverted ways, who often have to wait until I write something to know what I've been thinking about. My parents, Kevin and Linda; my sister and brother-in-law, Anne Marie and Tony; my three favorite people in the world, Maggie, Eliot, and Winston: thank you for caring about the questions I can't always articulate, the ideas I can't quite explain, and the vision of Christ's reconciliation and justice that I can't always see. Your curiosity kept me focused when I wasn't sure anyone else would be interested.

Finally, the Christian witness of Ida B. Wells has been a hilltop light guiding me through the fog of racial injustice and white supremacy. Her courage and faithfulness orient me when I get turned around. I earnestly hope this book, in some small way, honors her costly discipleship to our Savior.

WHAT TO READ NEXT

NOW WHAT?

ONE OF MY NOT-SO-HIDDEN AGENDAS in writing this book was to expose readers to authors they may have previously missed, especially authors of color. This is important to me because the topic of race is one that has been critically engaged with by people of color for much—much!—longer than most white people have even known to think about it. Over the years, almost everything important that I've learned about race and about being white—as well as how to reflect theologically on these things—has come through friends, mentors, and authors of color. Their lived and reflected-on realities have been indispensable components of my own rediscipleship. These friends and authors were under no obligation to share their experiences and insight with me and I'll always be grateful that they've done so.

Having said that, if you've found anything in this book helpful, I'd like to suggest some important InterVarsity Press titles written by authors of color. Each of these has much to offer anyone who is following Jesus into solidarity with the body of Christ.

- *Unsettling Truths*—Mark Charles and Soong-Chan Rah
- *True Story*—James Choung
- *Rethinking Incarceration*—Dominique DuBois Gilliard
- *Seeing Jesus in East Harlem*—José Humphreys
- *Prophetic Lament*—Soong-Chan Rah
- *Race and Place*—David P. Leong

- *Healing Racial Trauma*—Sheila Wise Rowe

- *The Heart of Racial Justice*—Brenda Salter McNeil and Rick Richardson

- *Roadmap to Reconciliation 2.0: Moving Communities into Unity, Wholeness and Justice*—Brenda Salter McNeil

- *A Sojourner's Truth*—Natasha Sistrunk Robinson

- *Beyond Colorblind*—Sarah Shin

- *Rescuing the Gospel from the Cowboys*—Richard Twiss

- *The Next Worship*—Sandra Maria Van Opstal

- *Welcoming the Stranger*—Matthew Soerens and Jenny Yang

- *Hermanas*—Natalia Kohn Rivera, Noemi Vega Quiñones, and Kristy Garza Robinson

- *Church Forsaken*—Jonathan Brooks

- *Raise Your Voice: Why We Stay Silent and How to Speak Up*—Kathy Khang

- *Birmingham Revolution: Martin Luther King Jr.'s Epic Challenge to the Church*—Edward Gilbreath

- *Can "White" People Be Saved? Triangulating Race, Theology, and Mission*—Edited by Love L. Sechrest, Johnny Ramírez-Johnson, and Amos Yong

- *Disunity in Christ: Uncovering the Hidden Forces That Keep Us Apart*—Christena Cleveland

NOTES

INTRODUCTION TO PART ONE: FROM CHEAP DIVERSITY . . .

[1]While we will primarily be dealing with race in this book, the realities of American life mean that ethnicity and culture are also an important part of any conversation about racial justice and reconciliation. In general terms, culture has to do with the shared beliefs, values, and practices of a social group while those who belong to a common ethnic group share a country of origin, language, or culture. Race, as we will see, is distinct from culture or ethnicity, though in America it overlaps with both, in that it exists as a human construction designed to privilege some while marginalizing others.

[2]Jennifer Harvey, *Dear White Christians: For Those Still Longing for Reconciliation* (Grand Rapids, MI: Eerdmans, 2014), 15. Kate Shellnutt, "Guess Who's Coming to Church: Multiracial Congregations Triple Among Protestants," *Christianity Today*, June 22, 2018, www.christianitytoday.com/news/2018/june/multiracial -congregations-triple-protestants-baylor-study.html. Korie L. Edwards, Brad Christerson, and Michael O. Emerson, "Race, Religious Organizations, and Integration," *The Annual Review of Sociology* 39 (May 24, 2013): 213, https://doi.org /10.1146/annurev-soc-071312-145636.

[3]When I refer to those Christians and their churches who exist outside the bounds of whiteness, I'm not suggesting that they are immune from the kinds of warped assumptions and destructive actions that, as we'll see, are a part of racial whiteness. Those who find themselves a part of an ethnic or racial or cultural minority in this country still must engage with the cultural majority. Rather, I'm asking us to remember the important differences between those of us who have experienced the relative protections of being the racial majority and those who have not.

1 DISCIPLED BY RACE

[1]Project Implicit, a collaboration between professors at universities around the country, has one of these implicit bias tests that can be accessed at implicit. harvard.edu/implicit/takeatest.html.

[2]Aaron Glantz and Emmanuel Martinez, "Kept Out," *Reveal*, February 15, 2018, www.revealnews.org/article/for-people-of-color-banks-are-shutting-the-door-to -homeownership/. Jamiles Lartey, "Median Wealth of Black Americans 'Will Fall to Zero by 2053,' Warns New Report," *The Guardian*, September 13, 2017, www.the guardian.com/inequality/2017/sep/13/median-wealth-of-black-americans-will

-fall-to-zero-by-2053-warns-new-report. Andrew Cohen, "What We've Learned About Racial Disparity in Policing Since Ferguson," *The Marshall Project*, August 10, 2015, https://www.themarshallproject.org/2014/11/19/what-we-ve-learned-about -racial-disparity-in-policing-since-ferguson. Amanda Holpuch, "Black Patients Half as Likely to Receive Pain Medication as White Patients, Study Finds," *The Guardian*, August 10, 2016, www.theguardian.com/science/2016/aug/10/black-patients -bias-prescriptions-pain-management-medicine-opioids. Linda Villarosa, "Why America's Black Mothers and Babies Are in a Life-or-Death Crisis," *New York Times Magazine*, April 11, 2018, www.nytimes.com/2018/04/11/magazine/black-mothers -babies-death-maternal-mortality.html.

[3]Dallas Willard, "Discipleship: For Super Christians Only?" *Christianity Today*, October 10, 1980, www.christianitytoday.com/ct/1980/october-10/discipleship-for -super-christians-only.html.

[4]Dallas Willard, *The Divine Conspiracy* (San Francisco: HarperCollins, 1997), 282.

[5]Augustine, *Confessions*, trans. F. J. Sheed, 2nd ed. (Indianapolis: Hackett Publishing Company, 2006), 64.

[6]Augustine, 3.

[7]James K. A. Smith, *Desiring the Kingdom: Worship, Worldview, and Cultural Formation* (Grand Rapids, MI: Baker Academic, 2009), 56.

[8]Smith, 80.

[9]Smith, 83.

[10]James K. A. Smith, *How (Not) to Be Secular: Reading Charles Taylor* (Grand Rapids, MI: Eerdmans, 2014), 143. Smith is quoting Charles Taylor here.

[11]Augustine, *Ten Homilies on the First Epistle of John to the Parthians*, trans. H. Browne (London: Aeterna, 2014), 44.

[12]Christopher Ingram, "Three Quarters of Whites Don't Have Any Non-White Friends," *Washington Post*, August 25, 2014, www.washingtonpost.com/news/wonk /wp/2014/08/25/three-quarters-of-whites-dont-have-any-non-white-friends /?utm_term=.b994b0930aa1.

[13]"In First Month, Views of Trump Are Already Strongly Felt, Deeply Polarized," *Pew Research Center*, February 16, 2017, www.people-press.org/2017/02/16/2 -views-of-trumps-executive-order-on-travel-restrictions/. Robert P. Jones, Daniel Cox, Rob Griffin, Molly Fisch-Friedman, and Alex Vandermaas-Peeler, "American Democracy in Crisis: The Challenges of Voter Knowledge, Participation, and Polarization," *PRRI*, June 17, 2018, www.prri.org/research/American-democracy -in-crisis-voters-midterms-trump-election-2018.

[14]James McWilliams, "Bryan Stevenson on What Well-Meaning White People Need to Know About Race," *Pacific Standard*, updated February 18, 2019, https:// psmag.com/magazine/bryan-stevenson-ps-interview.

[15]Eddie S. Glaude, *Democracy in Black* (New York: Crown Publishers, 2016), 55.

[16] Glaude, *Democracy in Black*, 56.

[17]Richard Rothstein, *The Color of Law: A Forgotten History of How Our Government Segregated America* (New York: Liveright Publishing Corporation, 2017).

2 CONCEALED BY RACE

[1]Campbell Roberson, "A Quiet Exodus: Why Black Worshipers Are Leaving White Evangelical Churches," *New York Times*, www.nytimes.com/2018/03/09/us/blacks-evangelical-churches.html.

[2]James Baldwin, "Nobody Knows My Name," in *Collected Essays*, ed. Toni Morrison (New York: Library of America, 1998), 200.

[3]Kate Shellnutt, "Guess Who's Coming to Church: Multiracial Congregations Triple Among Protestants," *Christianity Today*, June 22, 2018, www.christianity today.com/news/2018/june/multiracial-congregations-triple-protestants-baylor -study.html.

[4]Sarah Eekhoff Zylstra, "Surprise Change in How Multiethnic Churches Affect Race Views," *Christianity Today*, December 2, 2015, www.christianitytoday.com/ct /2015/december-web-only/surprise-shift-in-how-multiethnic-churches-affect -race-view.html.

[5]James Baldwin, "My Dungeon Shook," in *Collected Essays*, ed. Toni Morrison (New York: Library of America, 1998), 294.

[6]Michael Emerson and Christian Smith, *Divided by Faith: Evangelical Religion and the Problem of Race in America* (Oxford: Oxford University Press, 200), 7.

[7]Emerson and Smith, *Divided by Faith*, 76.

[8]Jennifer Harvey, *Dear White Christians: For Those Still Longing for Racial Recon- ciliation* (Grand Rapids, MI: Eerdmans, 2014), 19.

[9]Drew G. I. Hart, *Trouble I've Seen: Changing the Way the Church Views Racism* (Harrisonburg, VA: Herald Press, 2016), 28.

[10]Emerson and Smith, *Divided by Faith*, 90-91.

[11]Jacqueline Jones Royster, ed., *Southern Horrors and Other Writings: The Anti- Lynching Campaign of Ida B. Wells, 1829-1900* (Boston: Bedford/St. Martin's, 1997), 52.

[12]Royster, ed., *Southern Horrors*, 51.

[13]Ida B. Wells, letter dated January 1, 1886, The Ida B. Wells Papers 1884-1976, University of Chicago, www.lib.uchicago.edu/ead/pdf/ibwells-0008-009-01.pdf.

[14]Royster, ed., *Southern Horrors*, 140.

[15]Daniel Hill, *White Awake: An Honest Look at What It Means to Be White* (Downers Grove, IL: InterVarsity Press, 2017), 27.

[16]Harvey, *Dear White Christians*, 60-61.

3 WOUNDED BY RACE

[1]Austin Channing Brown, *I'm Still Here: Black Dignity in a World Made for Whiteness* (New York: Convergent Books, 2018), 154.

[2]Anthony Szczesiul, *The Southern Hospitality Myth: Ethics, Politics, Race, and American Memory* (Athens, GA: University of Georgia Press, 2017), 22.

[3]Dallas Willard, "Discipleship: For Super Christians Only?" *Christianity Today*, October 10, 1980, https://static1.squarespace.com/static/56fb268259827e51fccfabba /t/5d8f8d0ea1085f23a2c5fe2c/1569688848106/dwillard_discipleship_article.pdf.

[4]Ta-Nehisi Coates, *Between the World and Me* (New York: Spiegel and Grau, 2015), 10.

[5]James Baldwin, "On Being 'White' . . . and Other Lies," in *Collected Essays*, ed. Toni Morrison (New York: Library of America, 1998), 178.

[6]For some white people this can be an easier or more difficult reality to accept depending on the distance from their immigrant story. A white pastor recently told me that he struggled to see himself as racially privileged given the oppression suffered by his Polish-immigrant parents. Without taking anything away from his relatives' struggles, what I hoped this man would come to see is the access he and his children have to racial whiteness and the way this insulates them from the discrimination and oppression of racism.

[7]Coates, *Between the World*, 8.

[8]Ken Wytsma, *The Myth of Equality* (Downers Grove, IL: InterVarsity Press, 2017), 18.

[9]Eula Biss, *Notes from No Man's Land: American Essays* (Minneapolis: Graywolf Press, 2009), 32.

[10]Drew G. I. Hart, *Trouble I've Seen: Changing the Way the Church Views Racism* (Harrisonburg, VA: Herald Press, 2016), 46.

[11]Wendell Berry, *The Hidden Wound* (Berkeley, CA: Counterpoint, 1989), 4.

[12]Channing Brown, *I'm Still Here*, 89.

[13]Hart, *Trouble I've Seen*, 119.

[14]"Choice Words From Donald Trump, Presidential Candidate," *New York Times*, June 16, 2015, www.nytimes.com/politics/first-draft/2015/06/16/choice-words -from-donald-trump-presidential-candidate/.

[15]Chanequa Walker-Barnes, *Too Heavy a Yoke: Black Women and the Burden of Strength* (Eugene, OR: Cascade Books, 2014), 4.

[16]Walker-Barnes, *Too Heavy*, 5.

[17]Jeff Chang, *We Gon' Be Alright: Notes on Race and Resegregation* (New York: Picador, 2016), 146.

[18]Hart, *Trouble I've Seen*, 145.

[19]Berry, *Hidden Wound*, 6.

[20]Eula Biss, "White Debt," *New York Times Magazine*, December 2, 2015, www .nytimes.com/2015/12/06/magazine/white-debt.html.

[21]Channing Brown, *I'm Still Here*, 11.

[22]Frederick Douglass, *Narrative of the Life of Frederick Douglass, an American Slave* (New York: Literary Classics, 1994), 97.

[23]Gnenn Bracey and Wendy Moore, "'Race Tests': Racial Boundary Maintenance in White Evangelical Churches," *Sociological Inquiry* 87, no. 2 (May 2017): 282.

[24]Colleta Rhoads, "Not Even Safe at Church: Suffering from Our Ethnic Divisions," *Black in America / White in South Africa* (blog), March 26, 2018, http://collettarhoads .com/2018/03/26/not-even-safe-at-church-suffering-from-our-ethnic-divisions/.

[25]Berry, *Hidden Wound*, 19.

[26]Channing Brown, *I'm Still Here*, 179.

INTRODUCTION TO PART TWO: . . . TO TRUE SOLIDARITY

[1]James K. A. Smith, *Desiring the Kingdom* (Grand Rapids, MI: Baker Academic, 2009), 88.

[2]Drew G. I. Hart, *Trouble I've Seen: Changing the Way the Church Views Racism* (Harrisonburg, VA: Herald Press, 2016), 87.

4 PRACTICING TABLE FELLOWSHIP

[1]Theresa F. Latini, *The Church and the Crisis of Community* (Grand Rapids, MI: Eerdmans, 2001), 83.

[2]Simon Chan, *Liturgical Theology: The Church as Worshiping Community* (Downers Grove, IL: InterVarsity Press, 2006), 72.

[3]David Fitch, *Faithful Presence* (Downers Grove, IL: InterVarsity Press, 2016), 52.

[4]Fitch, *Faithful Presence*, 52.

[5]Robert E. Webber, *Ancient-Future Worship: Proclaiming and Enacting God's Narrative* (Grand Rapids, MI: Baker, 2008), 144.

[6]Latini, *Church and the Crisis*, 147.

5 PRACTICING KINGDOM PREACHING

[1]Frank A. Thomas, *They Like to Never Quit Praisin' God* (Cleveland, OH: Pilgrim Press, 1997), 4.

[2]Thomas, *Never Quit Praisin' God*, 3.

[3]Michael O. Emerson, *People of the Dream: Multiracial Congregations in the United States* (Princeton: Princeton University Press, 2006), 135.

[4]Ken Wytsma, *The Myth of Equality: Uncovering the Roots of Injustice and Privilege* (Downers Grove, IL: InterVarsity Press, 2017), 25-26.

[5]Michael Eric Dyson, *Tears We Cannot Stop: A Sermon to White America* (New York: St. Martin's Press, 2017), 44.

[6]Jennifer Harvey, *Dear White Christians: For Those Still Longing for Racial Reconciliation* (Grand Rapids, MI: Eerdmans, 2014), 47.

[7]"Findings," The Stanford Open Policing Project, accessed January 28, 2019, https://openpolicing.stanford.edu/findings/.

[8]Charles L. Campbell, *The Word Before the Powers: An Ethic of Preaching* (Louisville, KY: Westminster John Knox, 2002), 11.

[9]Campbell, *The Word Before the Powers*, 19.

[10]Michael Eric Dyson, *Tears We Cannot Stop: A Sermon to White America* (New York: St. Martin's Press, 2017), 96.

[11]James Baldwin, "My Dungeon Shook," in *Collected Essays*, ed. Toni Morrison (New York: Library of America, 1998), 293.

[12]Baldwin, "My Dungeon Shook," 292.

[13]Campbell, *Word Before the Powers*, 85.

[14]Campbell, *Word Before the Powers*, 183.

[15]Eddie S. Glaude, *Democracy in Black* (New York: Crown Publishers, 2016), 76.

[16]Mary Mitchell, "In Van Dyke Case, Jurors Should Remember Who's on Trial," *Chicago Sun Times*, October 4, 2018, https://chicago.suntimes.com/news/van-dyke -trial-laquan-mcdonald-demonized/.

[17]Glaude, *Democracy in Black*, 79.

[18]I published this address on my blog, and much of this section is paralleled there. "Do Not Conform," *David W. Swanson* (blog), May 2, 2018. https://dwswanson.com /2018/05/02/do-not-conform/.

[19]Marilynne Robinson, *Gilead* (New York: Farrar, Straus and Giroux, 2004), 36-37.

6 PRACTICING SUBVERSIVE LITURGIES

[1]Not all churches worship on Sundays, but for simplicity's sake I am pegging the weekly worship service to the day the church has historically gathered.

[2]James K. A. Smith, *Desiring the Kingdom: Worship, Worldview, and Cultural Formation* (Grand Rapids, MI: Baker Academic, 2009), 88.

[3]Sandra Van Opstal, *The Next Worship: Glorifying God in a Diverse World* (Downers Grove, IL: InterVarsity Press, 2016), 130.

[4]James K. A. Smith, *Imagining the Kingdom: How Worship Works* (Grand Rapids, MI: Baker Academic, 2013), 168.

[5]Joseph Cardinal Ratzinger, *The Spirit of the Liturgy* (San Francisco: Ignatius Press, 2000), 174.

[6]Ratzinger, *Spirit of the Liturgy*, 152.

[7]Ratzinger, *Spirit of the Liturgy*, 175.

[8]Van Opstal, *Next Worship*, 125. See also Smith, *Imagining the Kingdom*, 170-71.

[9]Simon Chan, *Liturgical Theology: The Church as Worshiping Community* (Downers Grove, IL: InterVarsity Press, 2006), 149.

[10] *The Covenant Book of Worship* (Chicago: Covenant Publications, 2003), 162.

[11] Chan, *Liturgical Theology*, 138.

[12] Smith, *Imagining the Kingdom*, 204.

[13] Smith, *Imagining the Kingdom*, 204.

[14] Ta-Nehisi Coates, "We Should Have Seen Trump Coming," *The Guardian*, September 29, 2017, www.theguardian.com/news/2017/sep/29/we-should-have-seen-trump-coming.

7 PRACTICING CHILDREN'S MINISTRY OF RECONCILIATION

[1] James Baldwin, "Down at the Cross," in *Collected Essays*, ed. Toni Morrison (New York: Library of America, 1998), 302.

[2] Jennifer Harvey, *Raising White Kids: Bringing Up Children in a Racially Unjust America* (Nashville: Abingdon, 2017), 40.

[3] Wendell Berry, *The Hidden Wound* (Berkeley, CA: Counterpoint, 1989), 3.

[4] Harvey, *Raising White Kids*, 235.

[5] Eddie S. Glaude, *Democracy in Black* (New York: Crown Publishers, 2016), 56.

[6] Po Bronson and Ashley Merryman, "Even Babies Discriminate: A Nurtureshock Excerpt," *Newsweek*, September 4, 2009, www.newsweek.com/even-babies-discriminate-nurtureshock-excerpt-79233.

[7] Harvey, *Raising White Kids*, 34.

[8] Margaret G. Hagerman, "White Progressive Parents and the Conundrum of Privilege," *Los Angeles Times*, September 30, 2018, www.latimes.com/opinion/op-ed/la-oe-hagerman-white-parents-20180930-story.html.

[9] Erica Minta Maxfield-Steele, "Making Space: Attending to the Spiritual Wisdom of Children," in *Story, Formation, and Culture: From Theory to Practice in Ministry with Children* (Eugene, OR: Pickwick Publications, 2018), 76.

[10] Michelle A. Clifton-Soderstrom and David D. Bjorlin, *Incorporating Children in Worship* (Eugene, OR: Cascade Books, 2014), 16.

[11] Vanderwell and Malefyt point to the Passover Feast in Exodus 12–13, the expectations that God's mighty deeds are told to future generations (Psalm 78:1-8), Jesus' parents bringing him to the temple for worship, and the baptisms of entire households in Acts as "the inclusion of the family as a unit before God." Howard Vanderwell and Normal de Waal Malefyt, "Worship that is Friendly to Children—Part 1," *Calvin Institute of Christian Worship*, accessed December 21, 2018, https://worship.calvin.edu/resources/resource-library/worship-that-is-friendly-to-children-part-1/.

[12] Clifton-Soderstrom and Bjorlin, *Incorporating Children*, 52.

[13] Marva Dawn, *Is It a Lost Cause?* (Grand Rapids, MI: Eerdmans, 1997), 33.

[14] La Verne Tolbert and Marilyn Brownlee, "The African American Church and Its Role in Nurturing the Spiritual Development of Children," in *Nurturing*

Children's Spirituality: Christian Perspective and Best Practices, ed. Holly Catterton Allen (Eugene, OR: Cascade Books, 2008), 328.

[15]Tolbert and Brownlee, "The African American Church," 203.

[16]Dawn, *Is It a Lost Cause?*, 131.

[17]Dawn, *Is It a Lost Cause?*, 74.

[18]Harvey, *Raising White Kids*.

8 PRACTICING PRESENCE

[1]Brenda Salter McNeil, *Roadmap to Reconciliation: Moving Communities into Unity, Wholeness and Justice* (Downers Grove, IL: InterVarsity Press, 2015), 23-24.

[2]Randy S. Woodley, *Shalom and the Community of Creation: An Indigenous Vision* (Grand Rapids, MI: Eerdmans, 2012), 120.

[3]David P. Leong, *Race and Place* (Downers Grove: InterVarsity Press, 2017) 35.

[4]Willie James Jennings, "Overcoming Racial Faith," *Divinity*, Spring 2015, 6, https://divinity.duke.edu/sites/divinity.duke.edu/files/divinity-magazine/Duke DivinityMag_Spring15.WEB_.compressed.pdf.

[5]Willie James Jennings, *The Christian Imagination: Theology and the Origins of Race* (New Haven: Yale, 2010), 32.

[6]Jennings, *The Christian Imagination*, 33.

[7]Jennings, *The Christian Imagination*, 43.

[8]"*Dum Diversas*," Doctrine of Discovery, accessed November 16, 2019, https:// doctrineofdiscovery.org/dum-diversas/.

[9]"*Dum Diversas*," 103.

[10]Woodley, *Shalom and the Community*, 52.

[11]Leong, *Race and Place*, 41.

[12]"Mapping Inequality: Redlining in New Deal America," accessed January 3, 2019, https://dsl.richmond.edu/panorama/redlining/#loc=4/36.71/-96.93&opacity=0.8.

[13]Jonathan Wilson-Hartgrove, *The Wisdom of Stability: Rooting Faith in a Mobile Culture* (Brewster, MA: Paraclete, 2010), 82.

[14]Wilson-Hartgrove, *The Wisdom of Stability*, 108.

[15]Brian Bantum, *The Death of Race: Building a New Christianity in a Racial World* (Minneapolis: Fortress Press, 2016), 157.

[16]Woodley, *Shalom and the Community*, 57.

9 PRACTICING SALVATION FROM SUPERIORITY

[1]"(1898) Rev. Francis J. Grimké, 'The Negro Will Never Acquiesce as Long as He Lives,'" BlackPast.org, January 29, 2007, https://blackpast.org/1898-reverend-francis -j-grimke-negro-will-never-acquiesce-long-he-lives.

[2]Martin Luther King, Jr., "Letter from a Birmingham Jail April 16, 1963," *African*

Studies Center—University of Pennsylvania, accessed January 8, 2019, www.africa
.upenn.edu/Articles_Gen/Letter_Birmingham.html.

[3]Dallas Willard, *The Divine Conspiracy* (San Francisco: HarperCollins, 1997), 305.

[4]Willard, *The Divine Conspiracy*, 305.

[5]James Choung, *True Story: A Christianity Worth Believing In* (Downers Grove, IL: InterVarsity Press, 2008), 198.

[6]Ashley Nellis, "The Color of Justice: Racial and Ethnic Disparity in State Prisons," *The Sentencing Project*, June 14, 2016, www.sentencingproject.org/publications/color -of-justice-racial-and-ethnic-disparity-in-state-prisons/.

[7]Michelle Alexander, *The New Jim Crow: Mass Incarceration in the Age of Colorblindness* (New York: New Press, 2010). Dominique Gilliard, *Rethinking Incarceration: Advocating for Justice That Restores* (Downers Grove, IL: InterVarsity Press, 2018).

[8]Willard, *The Divine Conspiracy*, 302.

[9]Michael Eric Dyson, *Tears We Cannot Stop: A Sermon to White America* (New York: St. Martin's Press, 2017), 203.

[10]John Teter, *Get the Word Out: How God Shapes and Sends His Witnesses* (Downers Grove, IL: InterVarsity Press, 2003), 58.

10 PRACTICING UNCOMMON FRIENDSHIP

[1]Brian Bantum, *The Death of Race: Building a New Christianity in a Racial World* (Minneapolis: Fortress Press, 2016), 102.

[2]Wendell Berry, *The Hidden Wound* (Berkeley, CA: Counterpoint, 1989), 78.

[3]Michael Emerson and Christian Smith, *Divided by Faith: Evangelical Religion and the Problem of Race in America* (Oxford: Oxford University Press, 200), 131.

[4]Brenda Salter McNeil, *Roadmap to Reconciliation: Moving Communities into Unity, Wholeness and Justice* (Downers Grove, IL: InterVarsity Press, 2015), 22.

[5]Sandra Van Opstal, *The Next Worship: Glorifying God in a Diverse World* (Downers Grove, IL: InterVarsity Press, 2016), 66.

[6]Daniel Hill, *White Awake: An Honest Look at What It Means to Be White* (Downers Grove, IL: InterVarsity Press, 2017).

[7]Hill, *White Awake*, 98.

[8]Van Opstal, *Next Worship*, 66.

[9]Michael Eric Dyson, *Tears We Cannot Stop: A Sermon to White America* (New York: St. Martin's Press, 2017), 206.

[10]Dyson, *Tears We Cannot Stop*, 207.

[11]Harvey, *Dear White Christians* (Grand Rapids, MI: Eerdmans, 2014), 170.

IVPRAXIS

EQUIPPING LEADERS FOR MINISTRY

"...TO EQUIP HIS PEOPLE FOR WORKS OF SERVICE,

SO THAT THE BODY OF CHRIST MAY BE BUILT UP."

EPHESIANS 4:12

God has called us to ministry. But it's not enough to have a vision for ministry if you don't have the practical skills for it. Nor is it enough to do the work of ministry if what you do is headed in the wrong direction. We need both vision *and* expertise for effective ministry. We need *praxis*.

Praxis puts theory into practice. It brings cutting-edge ministry expertise from visionary practitioners. You'll find sound biblical and theological foundations for ministry in the real world, with concrete examples for effective action and pastoral ministry. Praxis books are more than the "how to"—they're also the "why to." And because *being* is every bit as important as *doing*, Praxis attends to the inner life of the leader as well as the outer work of ministry. Feed your soul, and feed your ministry.

If you are called to ministry, you know you can't do it on your own. Let Praxis provide the companions you need to equip God's people for life in the kingdom.

www.ivpress.com/praxis